Israel's Eternal Covenant

Robert M. Pill

Israel's Eternal Covenant
Robert M. Pill

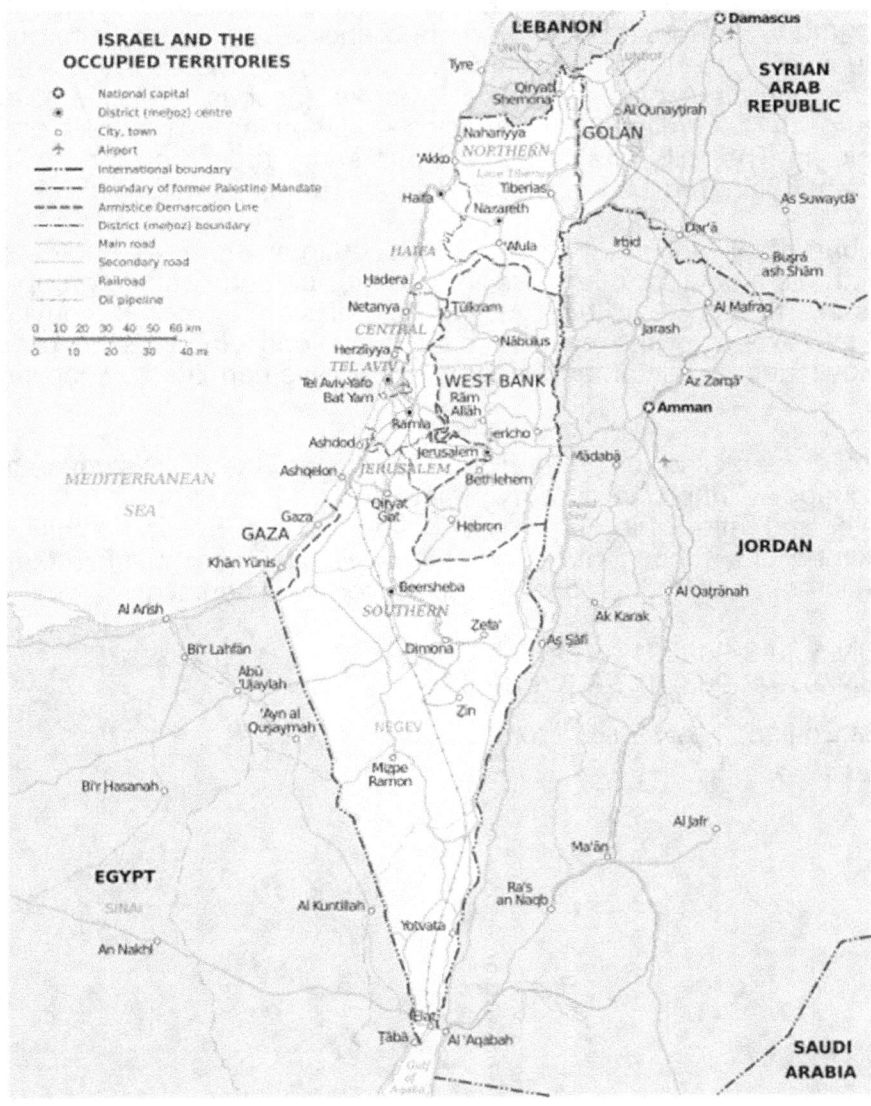

ISRAEL AND THE
OCCUPIED TERRITORIES

○   National capital
⊛   District (mehoz) centre
○   City, town
✈   Airport
━━━━   International boundary
━ ━ ━   Boundary of former Palestine Mandate
━ ━ ━   Armistice Demarcation Line
━ ━ ━   District (mehoz) boundary
━━━━   Main road
━━━━   Secondary road
┼━━━   Railroad
━ ━ ━   Oil pipeline

0 10 20 30 40 50 60 km
0   10   20   30   40 mi

First impression - November 2025
Published by Robert M. Pill
Israel's Eternal Covenant
Copyright © 2025 by Robert M. Pill, All Rights Reserved.

Book Typesetting by Robert M. Pill (using the LaTeX typesetting
language — https://www.latex-project.org/).
Cover and Title Page graphic attribution: un.org, Public domain, via
Wikimedia Commons, https://commons.wikimedia.org/wiki/File:Map
_of_Israel,_neighbours_and_occupied_territories-en.svg).

ISBN: 979-8-9882917-5-6 (Soft Cover)
ISBN: 979-8-9882917-6-3 (eBook)

First Edition: Year: 2025 Month:

12 11 10 9 8 7 6 5 4 3 2 1

דברים י:יב־יה

Deuteronomy 10:12-15

יב וְעַתָּה֙ יִשְׂרָאֵ֔ל מָ֚ה יְהֹוָ֣ה אֱלֹהֶ֔יךָ שֹׁאֵ֖ל
מֵעִמָּ֑ךְ כִּ֣י אִם־לְ֠יִרְאָ֠ה אֶת־יְהֹוָ֨ה אֱלֹהֶ֜יךָ לָלֶ֣כֶת
בְּכָל־דְּרָכָיו֙ וּלְאַהֲבָ֣ה אֹת֔וֹ וְלַֽעֲבֹד֙ אֶת־יְהֹוָ֣ה
אֱלֹהֶ֔יךָ בְּכָל־לְבָבְךָ֖ וּבְכָל־נַפְשֶֽׁךָ:

10 12 And now, Israel, what doth Yehovah
thy God require of thee, but to fear Yehovah
thy God, to walk in all His ways, and to love
Him, and to serve Yehovah thy God with all
thy heart and with all thy soul;

יג לִשְׁמֹ֞ר אֶת־מִצְוֺ֤ת יְהֹוָה֙ וְאֶת־חֻקֹּתָ֔יו אֲשֶׁ֛ר אָֽנֹכִ֥י
מְצַוְּךָ֖ הַיּ֑וֹם לְט֖וֹב לָֽךְ:

13 to keep the commandments of Yehovah,
and His statutes, which I command thee this
day, for thy good?

יד הֵ֚ן לַֽיהֹוָ֣ה אֱלֹהֶ֔יךָ הַשָּׁמַ֖יִם וּשְׁמֵ֣י הַשָּׁמָ֑יִם הָאָ֖רֶץ
וְכָל־אֲשֶׁר־בָּֽהּ:

14 Behold, unto Yehovah thy God belongeth
the heaven, and the heaven of heavens, the
earth, with all that therein is.

יה רַ֧ק בַּֽאֲבֹתֶ֛יךָ חָשַׁ֥ק יְהֹוָ֖ה לְאַֽהֲבָ֣ה אוֹתָ֑ם וַיִּבְחַ֞ר
בְּזַרְעָ֣ם אַֽחֲרֵיהֶ֗ם בָּכֶ֛ם מִכָּל־הָֽעַמִּ֖ים כַּיּ֥וֹם הַזֶּֽה:

15 Only Yehovah had a delight in thy fathers
to love them, and He chose their seed after
them, even you, above all peoples, as it is this
day. [Deuteronomy 10:12-15 The Pill Tanakh]

Table of Contents

לִבְרִית עוֹלָם
The Eternal Covenant

The nation of Israel was directly established by **The Creator of the Universe,** whose Name is יְהֹוָה[1] [Yehovah[2]]. As such, from its very beginnings Israel was intended to be under the leadership, influence and authority of the Almighty God!

יְהֹוָה [Yehovah] revealed to מֹשֶׁה Moses His personal Name, which He had not even made known to *His friend, Abraham!*

this is My name for ever,
and this is My memorial unto all generations.

יה וַיֹּאמֶר עוֹד אֱלֹהִים אֶל־מֹשֶׁה כֹּה־תֹאמַר
אֶל־בְּנֵי יִשְׂרָאֵל יְהֹוָה אֱלֹהֵי אֲבֹתֵיכֶם אֱלֹהֵי
אַבְרָהָם אֱלֹהֵי יִצְחָק וֵאלֹהֵי יַעֲקֹב שְׁלָחַנִי
אֲלֵיכֶם זֶה־שְּׁמִי לְעֹלָם וְזֶה זִכְרִי לְדֹר דֹּר:

[1] The name of God, in Hebrew, with vowel pointers indicating the correct pronunciation. יְהֹוָה, יְהֹוָה m.n. the proper name of God in the Bible, Tetragrammaton. [It prob. derives from הוה (= to be). The usual transliteration 'Jehovah' is based on the supposition that the Tetragrammaton is the imperfect Qal or Hiph'il of הוה and lit. means 'the one who is', 'the existing', resp. 'who calls into existence'. In reality, however, the pronunciation and literal meaning of the Tetragrammaton is unknown. cp. יָה [1].]
Ernest Klein, 'A Comprehensive Etymological Dictionary of the Hebrew Language for Readers of English' (CARTA, Jerusalem), p 255 (right column).
Ernest Klein, 'A Comprehensive Etymological Dictionary of the Hebrew Language for Readers of English', Sefaria, accessed 9 Mar 2021, https://www.sefaria.org/Klein_Dictionary

[2] Yehovah. The English transliteration of the name of God in Hebrew (יְהֹוָה). For more information, see Hebrew Voices #47 – A Disastrous Misunderstanding of the Name Yehovah (Posted on March 11, 2020 by Nehemia Gordon): "In Hebrew Voices, A Disastrous Understanding of the Name Yehovah, Nehemia Gordon explains the meaning of Yehovah, the mistake people make thinking it has to do with "destruction," and how Yahweh in Gnostic sources is the god of chaos. Listen to the short podcast, and then check out the detailed grammatical explanation below, of how we know Yehovah has nothing to do with the Hebrew word for "destruction."
Suzette wrote: "Forgive me, I was one of those people who knew just enough Hebrew to be dangerous... Thanks for the article!"."
Nehemia Gordon, 'Hebrew Voices #47 – A Disastrous Misunderstanding of the Name Yehovah', Nehemia's Wall, last modified 11 Mar 2020, https://www.nehemiaswall.com/disastrous-misunderstanding-yehovah

15 And God said moreover unto Moses: 'Thus shalt thou say unto the children of Israel: Yehovah, the God of your fathers, the God of Abraham, the God of Isaac, and the God of Jacob, hath sent me unto you; this is My name for ever, and this is My memorial unto all generations. [Exodus 3:15 The Pill Tanakh]

The nation of Israel began with the relationship between יְהֹוָה [Yehovah] and Abraham, established through a series of covenants sealing that relationship. The covenants made by יְהֹוָה [Yehovah] to Abraham and his descendants (aka Israel, sons of Abraham, Isaac and Jacob) are ETERNAL!

יב א וַיֹּאמֶר יְהוָה אֶל־אַבְרָם לֶךְ־לְךָ מֵאַרְצְךָ וּמִמּוֹלַדְתְּךָ וּמִבֵּית אָבִיךָ אֶל־הָאָרֶץ אֲשֶׁר אַרְאֶךָּ׃

12 1 Now Yehovah said unto Abram: 'Get thee out of thy country, and from thy kindred, and from thy father's house, unto the land that I will show thee.

ב וְאֶעֶשְׂךָ לְגוֹי גָּדוֹל וַאֲבָרֶכְךָ וַאֲגַדְּלָה שְׁמֶךָ וֶהְיֵה בְּרָכָה׃

2 And I will make of thee a great nation, and I will bless thee, and make thy name great; and be thou a blessing.

ג וַאֲבָרְכָה מְבָרְכֶיךָ וּמְקַלֶּלְךָ אָאֹר וְנִבְרְכוּ בְךָ כֹּל מִשְׁפְּחֹת הָאֲדָמָה׃

3 And I will bless them that bless thee, and him that curseth thee will I curse; and in thee shall all the families of the earth be blessed.' [Genesis 12:1-3 The Pill Tanakh]

יְהֹוָה [Yehovah] modified that covenant relationship as found in Genesis 17, changing the names of אַבְרָם Abram to אַבְרָהָם Abraham and שָׂרַי Sarai to שָׂרָה Sarah, and instituting the covenant of circumcision.

Of note, the promised child to be born to Abraham and Sarah was Isaac. **Isaac was the first son born under the covenant of circumcision.**   Abraham was circumcised at the age of 99. **The first son born under the covenant of circumcision — from a circumcised father was Isaac** — and his male seed after him!

יז א וַיְהִי אַבְרָם בֶּן־תִּשְׁעִים שָׁנָה וְתֵשַׁע שָׁנִים
וַיֵּרָא יְהֹוָה אֶל־אַבְרָם וַיֹּאמֶר אֵלָיו אֲנִי־אֵל שַׁדַּי
הִתְהַלֵּךְ לְפָנַי וֶהְיֵה תָמִים:

17 <u>1</u> And when Abram was ninety years old and nine, Yehovah appeared to Abram, and said unto him: 'I am God Almighty; walk before Me, and be thou wholehearted.

ב וְאֶתְּנָה בְרִיתִי בֵּינִי וּבֵינֶךָ וְאַרְבֶּה אוֹתְךָ בִּמְאֹד
מְאֹד:

<u>2</u> And I will make My covenant between Me and thee, and will multiply thee exceedingly.'

ג וַיִּפֹּל אַבְרָם עַל־פָּנָיו וַיְדַבֵּר אִתּוֹ אֱלֹהִים
לֵאמֹר:

<u>3</u> And Abram fell on his face; and God talked with him, saying:

ד אֲנִי הִנֵּה בְרִיתִי אִתָּךְ וְהָיִיתָ לְאַב הֲמוֹן גּוֹיִם:

<u>4</u> 'As for Me, behold, My covenant is with thee, and thou shalt be the father of a multitude of nations.

ה וְלֹא־יִקָּרֵא עוֹד אֶת־שִׁמְךָ אַבְרָם וְהָיָה שִׁמְךָ
אַבְרָהָם כִּי אַב־הֲמוֹן גּוֹיִם נְתַתִּיךָ:

5 Neither shall thy name any more be called Abram, but thy name shall be Abraham; for the father of a multitude of nations have I made thee.

ו וְהִפְרֵתִי אֹתְךָ בִּמְאֹד מְאֹד וּנְתַתִּיךָ לְגוֹיִם
וּמְלָכִים מִמְּךָ יֵצֵאוּ:

6 And I will make thee exceeding fruitful, and I will make nations of thee, and kings shall come out of thee.

ז וַהֲקִמֹתִי אֶת־בְּרִיתִי בֵּינִי וּבֵינֶךָ וּבֵין זַרְעֲךָ
אַחֲרֶיךָ לְדֹרֹתָם לִבְרִית עוֹלָם לִהְיוֹת לְךָ
לֵאלֹהִים וּלְזַרְעֲךָ אַחֲרֶיךָ:

7 And I will establish My covenant between Me and thee and thy seed after thee throughout their generations for an everlasting covenant, to be a God unto thee and to thy seed after thee.

ח וְנָתַתִּי לְךָ וּלְזַרְעֲךָ אַחֲרֶיךָ אֵת | אֶרֶץ מְגֻרֶיךָ
אֵת כָּל־אֶרֶץ כְּנַעַן לַאֲחֻזַּת עוֹלָם וְהָיִיתִי לָהֶם
לֵאלֹהִים:

8 And I will give unto thee, and to thy seed after thee, the land of thy sojournings, all the land of Canaan, for an everlasting possession; and I will be their God.'

ט וַיֹּאמֶר אֱלֹהִים אֶל־אַבְרָהָם וְאַתָּה אֶת־בְּרִיתִי
תִשְׁמֹר אַתָּה וְזַרְעֲךָ אַחֲרֶיךָ לְדֹרֹתָם:

<u>9</u> And God said unto Abraham: 'And as for thee, thou shalt keep My covenant, thou, and thy seed after thee throughout their generations.

י זֹאת בְּרִיתִי אֲשֶׁר תִּשְׁמְרוּ בֵּינִי וּבֵינֵיכֶם וּבֵין זַרְעֲךָ אַחֲרֶיךָ הִמּוֹל לָכֶם כָּל־זָכָר:

<u>10</u> This is My covenant, which ye shall keep, between Me and you and thy seed after thee: every male among you shall be circumcised.

יא וּנְמַלְתֶּם אֵת בְּשַׂר עָרְלַתְכֶם וְהָיָה לְאוֹת בְּרִית בֵּינִי וּבֵינֵיכֶם:

<u>11</u> And ye shall be circumcised in the flesh of your foreskin; and it shall be a token of a covenant betwixt Me and you.

יב וּבֶן־שְׁמֹנַת יָמִים יִמּוֹל לָכֶם כָּל־זָכָר לְדֹרֹתֵיכֶם יְלִיד בָּיִת וּמִקְנַת־כֶּסֶף מִכֹּל בֶּן־נֵכָר אֲשֶׁר לֹא מִזַּרְעֲךָ הוּא:

<u>12</u> And he that is eight days old shall be circumcised among you, every male throughout your generations, he that is born in the house, or bought with money of any foreigner, that is not of thy seed.

יג הִמּוֹל ׀ יִמּוֹל יְלִיד בֵּיתְךָ וּמִקְנַת כַּסְפֶּךָ וְהָיְתָה בְרִיתִי בִּבְשַׂרְכֶם לִבְרִית עוֹלָם:

<u>13</u> He that is born in thy house, and he that is bought with thy money, must needs be circumcised; and My covenant shall be in your flesh for an everlasting covenant.

יד֭ וְעָרֵ֣ל ׀ זָכָ֗ר אֲשֶׁ֤ר לֹֽא־יִמּוֹל֙ אֶת־בְּשַׂ֣ר עָרְלָת֔וֹ
וְנִכְרְתָ֛ה הַנֶּ֥פֶשׁ הַהִ֖וא מֵעַמֶּ֑יהָ אֶת־בְּרִיתִ֖י הֵפַֽר׃

14   And the uncircumcised male who is not circumcised in the flesh of his foreskin, that soul shall be cut off from his people; he hath broken My covenant.

יה֖ וַיֹּ֤אמֶר אֱלֹהִים֙ אֶל־אַבְרָהָ֔ם שָׂרַ֣י אִשְׁתְּךָ֔
לֹא־תִקְרָ֥א אֶת־שְׁמָ֖הּ שָׂרָ֑י כִּ֥י שָׂרָ֖ה שְׁמָֽהּ׃

15   And God said unto Abraham: 'As for Sarai thy wife, thou shalt not call her name Sarai, but Sarah shall her name be.

יו֖ וּבֵרַכְתִּ֣י אֹתָ֔הּ וְגַ֨ם נָתַ֧תִּי מִמֶּ֛נָּה לְךָ֖ בֵּ֑ן וּבֵרַכְתִּ֗יהָ
וְהָֽיְתָ֣ה לְגוֹיִ֔ם מַלְכֵ֥י עַמִּ֖ים מִמֶּ֥נָּה יִהְיֽוּ׃

16   And I will bless her, and moreover I will give thee a son of her; yea, I will bless her, and she shall be a mother of nations; kings of peoples shall be of her.' [Genesis 17:1-16 The Pill Tanakh]

The Torah itself declares that it was Moses who wrote it in a book about the time that it's events occurred!

לא֖ ט וַיִּכְתֹּ֣ב מֹשֶׁה֮ אֶת־הַתּוֹרָ֣ה הַזֹּאת֒ וַֽיִּתְּנָ֗הּ
אֶל־הַכֹּהֲנִים֙ בְּנֵ֣י לֵוִ֔י הַנֹּֽשְׂאִ֕ים אֶת־אֲר֖וֹן בְּרִ֣ית
יְהֹוָ֑ה וְאֶל־כָּל־זִקְנֵ֖י יִשְׂרָאֵֽל׃

31   9   And Moses wrote this Torah, and delivered it unto the priests the sons of Levi, that bore the ark of the covenant of Yehovah, and unto all the elders of Israel.

י֖ וַיְצַ֥ו מֹשֶׁ֖ה אוֹתָ֣ם לֵאמֹ֑ר מִקֵּ֣ץ ׀ שֶׁ֤בַע שָׁנִים֙ בְּמֹעֵד֙

שְׁנַת הַשְּׁמִטָּה בְּחַג הַסֻּכּוֹת:

<u>10</u> And Moses commanded them, saying: 'At the end of every seven years, in the set time of the year of release, in the feast of tabernacles,

יא   בְּבוֹא כָל־יִשְׂרָאֵל לֵרָאוֹת אֶת־פְּנֵי יְהֹוָה אֱלֹהֶיךָ בַּמָּקוֹם אֲשֶׁר יִבְחָר תִּקְרָא אֶת־הַתּוֹרָה הַזֹּאת נֶגֶד כָּל־יִשְׂרָאֵל בְּאָזְנֵיהֶם:

<u>11</u> when all Israel is come to appear before Yehovah thy God in the place which He shall choose, thou shalt read this Torah before all Israel in their hearing.

יב   הַקְהֵל אֶת־הָעָם הָאֲנָשִׁים וְהַנָּשִׁים וְהַטַּף וְגֵרְךָ אֲשֶׁר בִּשְׁעָרֶיךָ לְמַעַן יִשְׁמְעוּ וּלְמַעַן יִלְמְדוּ וְיָרְאוּ אֶת־יְהֹוָה אֱלֹהֵיכֶם וְשָׁמְרוּ לַעֲשׂוֹת אֶת־כָּל־דִּבְרֵי הַתּוֹרָה הַזֹּאת:

<u>12</u> Assemble the people, the men and the women and the little ones, and thy stranger that is within thy gates, that they may hear, and that they may learn, and fear Yehovah your God, and observe to do all the words of this Torah;

יג   וּבְנֵיהֶם אֲשֶׁר לֹא־יָדְעוּ יִשְׁמְעוּ וְלָמְדוּ לְיִרְאָה אֶת־יְהֹוָה אֱלֹהֵיכֶם כָּל־הַיָּמִים אֲשֶׁר אַתֶּם חַיִּים עַל־הָאֲדָמָה אֲשֶׁר אַתֶּם עֹבְרִים אֶת־הַיַּרְדֵּן שָׁמָּה לְרִשְׁתָּהּ:

<u>13</u> and that their children, who have not known, may hear, and learn to fear Yehovah your God, as long as ye live in the land

whither ye go over the Jordan to possess it.'
[Deuteronomy 31:9-13 The Pill Tanakh]

לג א אֵ֣לֶּה מַסְעֵ֣י בְנֵֽי־יִשְׂרָאֵ֗ל אֲשֶׁ֥ר יָצְא֛וּ מֵאֶ֥רֶץ
מִצְרַ֖יִם לְצִבְאֹתָ֑ם בְּיַד־מֹשֶׁ֥ה וְאַהֲרֹֽן׃

33 1 These are the stages of the children
of Israel, by which they went forth out of the
land of Egypt by their hosts under the hand of
Moses and Aaron.

ב וַיִּכְתֹּ֨ב מֹשֶׁ֜ה אֶת־מוֹצָאֵיהֶ֛ם לְמַסְעֵיהֶ֖ם עַל־פִּ֣י
יְהוָ֑ה וְאֵ֥לֶּה מַסְעֵיהֶ֖ם לְמוֹצָאֵיהֶֽם׃

2 And Moses wrote their goings forth, stage
by stage, by the commandment of Yehovah;
and these are their stages at their goings forth.
[Numbers 33:1-2 The Pill Tanakh]

**I began this introductory chapter with the idea that
the nation of Israel was established by the Almighty
God, the creator of the universe, who disclosed His
Name to Moses as יְהֹוָה [Yehovah].**

**I wanted to establish that the Covenant Of
Circumcision that יְהֹוָה [Yehovah] made with
Abraham and his descendants was for all time
— Eternal: לִבְרִית עוֹלָם an everlasting covenant!**

הַכֹּהֵן הַגָּדוֹל

The Cohen Gadol

HIGH PRIEST IN ROBES AND BREASTPLATE.
—*Lev.* viii, 8, 1

According to the Jewish Scriptures, **as descendants of Abraham, Isaac and Jacob, the nation of Israel began under the leadership of Moses, its first major prophet.** Following Moses, Israel was lead by its Judges, Kings and Prophets.

The office of the High Priest was instituted during the time that the children of Israel wandered in the wilderness, after escaping from Egypt. Aaron, Moses's older brother, was anointed to be the first High Priest, known in Hebrew as הַכֹּהֵן הַגָּדוֹל, the Cohen Gadol.

---

[1]Free-images.com, 'lev 8 high priest,' accessed 27 May 2025, https://free-images.com/display/lev_8_high_priest.html.
Note from Free-images.com, ''This image was acquired from Wikimedia (https://commons.wikimedia.org/wiki/File:LEV_8-_High_priest_in_robes_and_breastplate.jpg). It was marked as Public Domain or CC0 and is free to use. To verify, go to the source and check the information there.''

The governance of ancient Israel was established within a religious system embodied under the office of the הַכֹּהֵן הַגָּדוֹל, the Cohen Gadol. The codification of laws, statutes and ordinances defined the nation's core foundation.

The office of a High Priest was intended to be a **lifetime appointment.**   Only when a High Priest died was a successor appointed — from a male descendant from the line of Aaron. According to the Scriptures, only "Aaronic Priests," — sons of Aaron and their sons were eligible to become a High Priest. **Succession was always paternal.**   The father always had to be the son of a previous male descendant from the line of Aaron!

כה ‏י‎ וַיְדַבֵּר יְהוָה אֶל־מֹשֶׁה לֵּאמֹר:

25 10 And Yehovah spoke unto Moses, saying:

‏יא‎ פִּינְחָס בֶּן־אֶלְעָזָר בֶּן־אַהֲרֹן הַכֹּהֵן הֵשִׁיב אֶת־חֲמָתִי מֵעַל בְּנֵי־יִשְׂרָאֵל בְּקַנְאוֹ אֶת־קִנְאָתִי בְּתוֹכָם וְלֹא־כִלִּיתִי אֶת־בְּנֵי־יִשְׂרָאֵל בְּקִנְאָתִי:

11 'Phinehas, the son of Eleazar, the son of Aaron the priest, hath turned My wrath away from the children of Israel, in that he was very jealous for My sake among them, so that I consumed not the children of Israel in My jealousy.

‏יב‎ לָכֵן אֱמֹר הִנְנִי נֹתֵן לוֹ אֶת־בְּרִיתִי שָׁלוֹם:

12 Wherefore say: Behold, I give unto him My covenant of peace;

‏יג‎ וְהָיְתָה לּוֹ וּלְזַרְעוֹ אַחֲרָיו בְּרִית כְּהֻנַּת עוֹלָם תַּחַת אֲשֶׁר קִנֵּא לֵאלֹהָיו וַיְכַפֵּר עַל־בְּנֵי יִשְׂרָאֵל:

<u>13</u> and it shall be unto him, and to his seed after him, the covenant of an everlasting priesthood; because he was jealous for his God, and made atonement for the children of Israel.' [Numbers 25:10-13 The Pill Tanakh]

In spite of having a foundation of laws, statutes and ordinances, the nation never operated fully under the **exclusive** authority of the office of the High Priest, הַכֹּהֵן הַגָּדוֹל, the Cohen Gadol.

When I first gave consideration to the idea of the Jewish High Priest, my thoughts gave rise to a question, *"Why was the office of the High Priest suspended?"* [2]

As I pondered that question, I thought about the time of the last High Priests in Israel, which appeared to be at the time of the first century C.E. (Common Era, aka AD).

At about that time I remembered reading some of the New Testament passages concerning Caiaphas:

<u>49</u> And one of them, named Caiaphas, being the high priest that same year, said unto them, Ye know nothing at all,
<u>50</u> Nor consider that it is expedient for us, that one man should die for the people, and that the whole nation perish not.
<u>51</u> And this spake he not of himself: but being high priest that year, he prophesied that Jesus should die for that nation; [John 11:49-51 KJV]

What? "...being the high priest <u>that same year</u>;"

How does that apply to High Priest succession as defined in the Torah, when a High Priest died and was succeeded by another

---

[2]After many years, beginning when the first Temple was destroyed and burned by Nebuchadnezzar until the starting of its rebuilding by Ezra and Nehemia (Jeremiah said that for 70 years Jerusalem would be unbuilt until 49 years after the order was proclaimed in Daniel 9:25). Also, during the time of Maccabees, the Temple was polluted by the Greeks and services suspended. Moreover, Herod's beautified Temple was destroyed by the Romans in 70 A.D.

male descendant of Aaron?

It is understood that Caiaphas was appointed by the Roman authorities, not through the Torah defined process.[3]

Were there other times when this sort of thing occurred? Unfortunately, the answer is, "Yes!"

During the time of the Maccabees the office of the High Priest was also usurped!

The Hasmoneans Usurped the High Priesthood from the Oniads

The family of Onias long controlled the high priesthood before the persecution of Antiochus IV and the Hasmoneans' ("Maccabees'") rebellion. When the dust settled, the Hasmoneans found themselves in charge of the priesthood and the Oniads had relocated to Egypt. 1 Maccabees, a pro-Hasmonean work, defends the legitimacy of the Hasmonean accession to the high priesthood, and the fact that it went to the family of Judah Maccabee's brother, Simon.

...

---

[3] In 18 CE, the Roman governor, Valerius Gratus, deposed Simon son of Camithus as the High Priest, and appointed Caiaphas to serve in this role.[1] Caiaphas was the son-in-law of Annas (Jn 18:13), a powerful man who had served as High Priest from 6–15 CE. Even after Annas was deposed, he retained considerable influence as five of his sons[2], and his son-in-law, Caiaphas, all served as the High Priest at various times. This is reflected in the fact that, after Jesus was arrested, he was taken first to Annas (Jn 18:13) and then to Caiaphas (Jn 18:24).

According to Josephus, his given name was "Joseph, who was also called Caiaphas."[3] He served as High Priest for a notably long period; when Gratus was succeeded by Pontius Pilate, Caiaphas remained in office. Both he and Pontius Pilate were eventually deposed by Lucius Vitellius, the governor of Syria, in 37 CE.[4]

Bryan Windle, 'Caiaphas: An Archaeological Biography,' BIBLE ARCHAEOLOGY REPORT, modified 17 Apr 2025, https://biblearchaeologyreport.com/2025/04/17/caiaphas-an-archaeological-biography/.

And yet, Yoḥanan the father of Mattathias was not the high priest Yoḥanan known in Greek sources as Onias (Heb. Ḥonyo), a nickname for Yoḥanan Indeed, Mattathias was not a scion of a high priestly family, and justifying the fact that his sons and grandsons ended up with the high priesthood, which was then the equivalent of ruling Judea, is the focus and point of the Hasmoneans' court history, 1 Maccabees. [4]

Was the Office of High Priest—Compromised?

It would appear to be so! — Especially after the destruction of Jerusalem by Nebchadnezzar, the office of the High Priest was not quite as well ordered as previously.

—Biblical Data:
Aaron, though he is but rarely called "the great priest," being generally simply designated "as ha- kohen" (the priest), was the first incumbent of the office, to which he was appointed by God (Ex. xxviii. 1, 2; xxix. 4, 5). The succession was to be through one of his sons, and was to remain in his own family (Lev. vi. 15; comp. Josephus, "Ant." xx. 10, § 1). Failing a son, the office devolved upon the brother next of age: such appears to have been the practise in the Maccabean period. In the time of ELI, however (I Sam. ii. 23), the office passed to the collateral branch of Ithamar (see Eleazar). But Solomon is reported to have deposed Abiathar, and to have appointed

---

[4]Prof. Daniel R. Schwartz, 'The Hasmoneans Usurped the High Priesthood from the Oniads,' The Torah, accessed 13 June 2025, https://www.thetorah.com/article/the-hasmoneans-usurped-the-high-priesthood-from-the-oniads

Zadok, a descendant of Eleazar, in his stead (I Kings ii. 35; I Chron. xxiv. 2, 3). After the Exile, the succession seems to have been, at first, in a direct line from father to son; but later the civil authorities arrogated to themselves the right of appointment. Antiochus IV., Epiphanes, for instance, deposed Onias III. in favor of Jason, who was followed by Menelaus (Josephus, "Ant." xii. 5, § 1; II Macc. iii. 4, iv. 23).

Herod nominated no less than six high priests; Archelaus, two. The Roman legate Quirinius and his successors exercised the right of appointment, as did Agrippa I., Herod of Chalcis, and Agrippa II. Even the people occasionally elected candidates to the office. The high priests before the Exile were, it seems, appointed for life (comp. Num. xxxv. 25, 28); in fact, from Aaron to the Captivity the number of the high priests was not greater than during the sixty years preceding the fall of the Second Temple.
...

List of High Priests.

1.	Aaron
2.	Eleazar
3.	Phinehas
4.	Abishua
5.	Bukki
6.	Uzzi (I Chron. vi. 3-5)

With Eli the high-priesthood passes from the line of Eleazar to that of Ithamar:

	Old Testament.	Josephus.
7.	Eli	Eli
8.	Ahitub (I Chron.ix. 11)	Ahitub
9.	Ahiah (I Sam. xiv. 3)	Ahiah
10.	Ahimelech (I Sam. xxi. 1)	Ahimelech
11.	Abiathar (I Sam. xxxiii. 6)	Abiathar ("Ant." v. 11., § 5

From Solomon to the Captivity.
(With Zadok the line of Eleazar reappears.)

	Old Testament.	Josephus.	Seder 'Olam Zuṭa.
12.	Zadok (I Kings ii. 35)	Zadok	Zadok
13.	Ahimaaz (II Sam. xv. 36)	Ahimaaz	Ahimaaz
14.	Azariah (I Kings iv. 2)	Azariah	Azariah
15.	....	Joran	Joash
16.	Jehoiarib (I Chron. ix. 10)	Jesus	Joarib
17.	....	Axiomar	Jehoshaphat
18.	Jehoiada (II Kings xi. 4)	....	Joiada
19.	....	Phideas	Pedaiah
20.	....	Sudeas	Zedekiah
21.	Azariah II. (II Chron. xxvi. 17)	Joel	Joel
22.	....	Jotham	Jotham
23.	Urijah (II Kings xvi. 10)	Uriah	Uriah
24.	Azariah III. (II Chron. xxxi. 10)	Neriah	Neriah
25.	....	Odeas	Hoshaiah
26.	Shallum (I Chron. vi. 12)	Shallum	Shallum
27.	Hilkiah (II Kings xxii. 4)	Hilkiah	Hilkiah
28.	Azariah IV. (I Chron. vi. 13)	"	Azariah
29.	Seraiah (II Kings xxv. 18)	Sareas	Zeraiah
30.	Jehozadak (I Chron. vi. 14)	Josedek	Jehozadak

Continued on next page

Old Testament.	Josephus.	Seder 'Olam Zuṭa.

From the Captivity to Herod.

	Old Testament.	Josephus.
31.	Jeshua (Hag. i. 1)	Jesus ("Ant." xi. 3, § 10)
32.	Joiakim (Neh. xii. 10)	Joiakim ("B. J." xi. 5, § 1)
33.	Eliashib (Neh. iii. 1)	Eliashib ("B. J." xi. 5, § 5)
34.	Joiada (Neh. xii. 10, 22)	Judas ("Ant." xi. 7, § 1)
35.	Johanan (Neh. xii. 22)	Joannes ("Ant." xi. 7., § 1)
36.	Jaddua (Neh. xii. 22)	Jaddus ("Ant." xi. 7, § 2)
37.	....	Onias I. ("Ant." xii. 2, § 5)

	Apocrypha..	Josephus ("Antiquities").
38.	Simon I. (Ecclus. [Sirach] 4, 1)	Simon the Just (xii. 2, § 5)
39.	....	Eleazar (xii. 2, § 5)
40.	....	Manasseh (xii. 4, § 1)
41.	....	Onias II. (xii. 4, § 1)
42.	....	Simon II. (xii. 4, § 10)
43.	Onias (I Macc. xii. 7)	Onias III. (xii. 4, § 10)
44.	Jason (II Macc. iv. 7)	Jesus (xii. 5, § 1)
45.	Menelaus (II Macc. iv. 27)	Onias, called Menelaus (xii. 5, § 1)
46.	Alcimus (I Macc. vii. 5)	Alcimus (xii. 9, § 7)
47.	Jonathan (I Macc. ix. 28)	Jonathan (xiii. 2, § 2)
48.	Simon (the Prince) (I Macc. xiv. 46)	Simon (xiii. 6, § 7)
49.	John (I Macc. xvi. 23)	John Hyrcanus (xiii. 8, § 1)
50.	....	Aristobulus I. (xiii. 9, § 1)
51.	....	Alexander Jannæus (xiii. 12, § 1)
52.	....	Hyrcanus II. (xiii. 16, § 2)
53.	....	Aristobulus II. (xv. 1, § 2)
54.	....	Hyrcanus II. (restored) (xiv. 4, 4)
55.	....	Antigone (xiv. 14, § 3)
56.	....	Hananeel (xv. 2, § 4)

From Herod to the Destruction of the Temple.
Josephus ("Antiquities")
(Under Herod.

56. | Hananeel
57. | Aristobulus III. (xv. 3, §§ 1, 3)
     | (Hananeel reappointed; xv. 3, § 3)
58. | Jesus, son of Phabet (xv. 9, § 3)
59. | Simon, son of Bœthus (perhaps Bœthus himself; xv.
     | 9, § 3; xvii. 4, § 2)
60. | Mattathias, son of Theophilus (xvii. 6, § 4)
     | Joseph, son of Ellem (one day; xvii. 6, § 4; see Grätz
     | in "Monatsschrift," 1881, pp. 51 et seq.)
61. | Joazar, son of Bœthus (xvii. 6, § 4)
     | (Under Archeiaus.)
62. | Eleazar, son of Bœthus (xvii. 13, § 1)
63. | Jesus, son of Sie (Σιε; xvii. 13, § 1)
     | (Joazar reappointed; xviii. 1. § 1; 2, § 1)
     | (Under Quirinius.)
64. | Ananus, son of Seth (xviii. 2, § 2; Luke iii. 2)
     | (Under Valorius Gratus.)
65. | Ismael, son of Phabi (xviii. 2, § 2)
66. | Eleazar, son of Ananus (xviii. 2, § 2)
67. | Simon, son of Camithus (xviii. 2, § 2)
68. | Joseph (called "Caiaphas" (xviii. 2, § 2; 4, § 3; Matt.
     | xxvi. 3, 57)
     | (Under Vitellius.)
69. | Jonathan, son of Ananus (xviii. 4, § 3; "B. J." ii. 12,
     | §§ 5-6; 13, § 3)
70. | Theophilus, son of Ananus (xviii. 5, § 3)
     | (Under Agrippa.)
71. | Simon, or Cantheras, son of Bœthus (xix. 6, § 2; see
     | Grätz., "Gesch." 4th ed., iii. 739-746)
72. | Mattathias, son of Ananus (xix. 6, § 4)
73. | Elioneus, son of Cantheras (xix. 8, § 1; Parah iii. 5)
     | (Under Herod of Chalcis.)
74. | Joseph, son of Cainus (xx. 1, § 3)
     | [Perhaps Ishmael (iii. 15, § 13) should be placed
     | here.]
75. | Ananias, son of Nebedeus (xx. 5, § 2; Derenbourg,
     | "Hist." p. 233)
     | (Jonathan restored; xx. 8, § 5)
     | (Under Agrippa II.)
76. | Ishmael, son of Fabi (xx. 8, §§ 8, 11; Parah iii. 5;
     | Sotah ix. 5; Derenbourg, "Hist." pp. 232-235)

77. Joseph Cabi, son of Simon (xx. 8, § 11)
78. Ananus, son of Ananus (xx. 9, § 1)
79. Jesus, son of Damneus (xx. 9, § 1; "B. J." vi. 2, § 2)
80. Jesus, son of Gamaliel (xx. 9, §§ 4, 7; Yeb. vi. 4; an instance in which a priest betrothed to a widow before his elevation was permitted to marry her afterward; Derenbourg, "Hist." p. 248)
81. Mattathias, son of Theophilus (xx. 9, § 7; "B. J." vi. 2, § 2; Grätz, in "Monatsschrift," 1881, pp. 62-64; idem, "Gesch." 4th ed., iii. 750 et seq.)
82. Phinehas, son of Samuel, appointed by the people during the war (xx. 10, § 1; "B. J." iv. 3, § 8; see Derenbourg, "Hist." p. 269)
[A man altogether unworthy.]

Josephus enumerates only fifty-two pontificates under the Second Temple, omitting the second appointments of Hyrcanus II., Hananeel, and Joazar.[5]

A Cohen Gadol
In A Third Temple In Yerushalam?

The Temple Institute is dedicated to every aspect of the Holy Temple of Jerusalem, and the central role it fulfilled, and will once again fulfill, in the spiritual well-being of both Israel and all the nations of the world. The Institute's work touches upon the history of the Holy Temple's past, an understanding of the present day, and the Divine promise of Israel's future. The Institute's activities include education, research, and development. The Temple Institute's ultimate goal is to see Israel rebuild the Holy Temple on Mount Moriah in Jerusalem, in accord with the Biblical commandments. It is of primary importance to educate about the great significance of the Holy Temple and Mount Moriah, the Temple Mount in Jerusalem, the only site in the world that is considered holy by the Jewish people, and the only

---

[5]Emil G. Hirsch, High Priest, JewishEncyclopedia, accessed 25 June 2025, https://www.jewishencyclopedia.com/articles/7689-high-priest

site in the world which G-d chose to rest His presence through the establishment of the Holy Temple.

The Temple Institute (in Hebrew, *Machon HaMikdash*), founded in 1987, is a non-profit educational and religious organization located in the Jewish quarter of Jerusalem's Old City. The Institute is dedicated to every aspect of the Biblical commandment to build the Holy Temple of G-d on Mount Moriah in Jerusalem. Our short-term goal is to rekindle the flame of the Holy Temple in the hearts of mankind through education. Our long-term goal is to do all in our limited power to bring about the building of the Holy Temple in our time. Thus, the Institute's efforts include raising public awareness about the Holy Temple, and the central role that it occupies in the spiritual life of mankind. The many areas of activities conducted by the Institute combine research, seminars, publications, and conferences, as well as the production of educational materials.

The major focus of the Institute is its efforts towards the beginning of the actual rebuilding of the Holy Temple. Towards this end, the Institute has begun to restore and construct the sacred vessels for the service of the Holy Temple. These vessels, which G-d commanded Israel to create, can be seen today at our exhibition in Jerusalem's Old City Jewish Quarter. They are made according to the exact specifications of the Bible, and have been constructed from the original source materials, such as gold, copper, silver and wood. These are authentic, accurate vessels, not merely replicas or models. All of these items are fit and ready for use in the service of the Holy Temple. Among the many items featured in the exhibition are musical instruments played by the Levitical choir, the golden crown of the High Priest, and gold and silver vessels used in the incense and sacrificial services. After many years of effort and toil, the Institute has completed the three most important and central vessels of the Divine service: the seven-branched candelabra, or Menorah, made of pure gold; the golden Incense Altar, and the golden Table of the Showbread. Other completed projects include the sacred uniform of the Kohen Gadol, the High Priest. This project was the culmination of years of study and research. The High Priest's *Choshen* (Breastplate), *Ephod* and the *tzitz* have been completed. All these and more can be seen at the ***Temple Institute Museum.*** [6]

The Temple Institute in Yerushalam has been in the process of preparing for an eventual rebuilding of the Temple by creating all priestly accoutrements. Morevoer, a nascent Sanhedrin has already chosen a candidate to perform the duties of the High Priest!

Rabbi Baruch Kahane

A significant step was recently taken towards reinstating the Temple service when the nascent Sanhedrin selected Rabbi Baruch Kahane as the next Kohen Gadol (high priest). The selection was made as a precaution for Yom Kippur. If the political conditions should change, allowing the Jews access to the Temple Mount, they will be required by Torah law to bring the sacrifices. Rabbi Kahane is

[6]TEMPLE INSTITUTE, 'ABOUT THE TEMPLE INSTITUTE', accessed 8 Sep 2025, https://templeinstitute.org/about-us/

confident that if that should happen, Temple service could begin in less than one week.

Rabbi Kahane is a prominent scholar, knowledgeable in the complicated laws pertaining to the subject of the Temple Service. He is part of the Halacha Berurah Institute, established by Rabbi Avraham Isaac HaCohen Kook, the first Chief Rabbi of Israel, which deals with the elucidation of Jewish law from its Talmudic sources (Oral Law) and commentaries. He has played a prominent role in all the reenactments of the Temple services performed to date.

This year has already seen much Temple-oriented activity: the Temple Institute has created a registry of kohanim; established a school for educating men of the priestly class in the details of the Temple service; and performed reenactments on all the holidays, including the especially significant Passover sacrifice. [7]

As you may see from the above article, there is an effort in our times to reestablish הַכֹּהֵן הַגָּדוֹל — the Cohen Gadol.

הַכֹּהֵן הַגָּדוֹל — the Cohen Gadol was established in the infancy of the nation of Israel. It appears that it was always intended to function along with judges, kings and prophets.

---

[7] Adam Eliyahu Berkowitz, 'Sanhedrin Appoints High Priest in Preparation for Third Temple', Israel365News, last updated 29 Aug 2016, https://israel365news.com/310069/sanhedrin-appoints-high-priest-preparation-third-temple/

Abrahamic Religion

Two Definitions Of Religion

religion noun

1 : a personal set or institutionalized system of religious attitudes, beliefs, and practices

2 a (1) : the service and worship of God or the supernatural

(2) : commitment or devotion to religious faith or observance

b : the state of a religious

I a nun in her 20th year of *religion*

3 : a cause, principle or system of beliefs held to with ardor and faith

4 archaic : scrupulous conformity : CONSCIENTIOUSNESS[1]

religion, human beings' relation to that which they regard as holy, sacred, absolute, spiritual, divine, or worthy of especial reverence. It is also commonly regarded as consisting of the way people deal with ultimate concerns about their lives and their fate after death. In many traditions, this relation and these concerns are expressed in terms of one's relationship with or attitude toward gods or spirits; in more humanistic or naturalistic forms of religion, they are expressed in terms of one's relationship with or attitudes toward the broader human community or the natural world. In many religions, texts are deemed to have scriptural status, and people are esteemed to be invested with spiritual or moral authority. Believers and worshippers participate in and are often enjoined to perform devotional or contemplative practices such as prayer, meditation, or particular rituals. Worship, moral conduct, right belief, and participation in religious institutions are among the constituent elements of the religious life.[2]

[1] Merriam-Webster Dictionary, 'religion,' accessed 16 Jul 2025, https://www.merriam-webster.com/dictionary/religion

[2] The Editors of Encyclopaedia Britannica, 'religion,' Last Updated 27 June 2025, https://www.britannica.com/topic/religion

Three Religions, One God

Three of the major religions were born in the Middle East. Judaism, Christianity, and Islam all recognize Abraham as their first prophet, so they are called the Abrahamic religions.

Jews believe in one god and his prophets, especially Moses.   Jews do not believe in Jesus and Muhammad.

Judaism emphasizes actions more than beliefs. Jewish law is written in the Torah and the Talmud, covering rituals, diet, marriage, and inheritance. Major holidays include Yom Kippur (the Day of Atonement) and Passover, with its seder meal (freedom feast).

Christians believe that God is revealed through the Father, the Son (Jesus Christ), and the Holy Spirit. Jesus was born to the Virgin Mary (celebrated at Christmas) and came to Earth to offer redemption for people's sins.   After Jesus was executed by the Romans, Christians believe he rose from the dead and ascended into heaven (celebrated at Easter).

Christians believe in an afterlife with rewards in heaven and punishment in hell.

Christians believe that the ritualistic Jewish law was replaced by a universal gospel for all humanity and the Christian teaching, "Love thy neighbor as thyself."

Muslims believe that Allah (Arabic for God) sent His revelation, the Quran, to the prophet Muhammad to declare it to mankind. The Quran tells Muslims to worship one god, and it explains how they should treat others.

Observant Muslims practice five principles: orally declaring their faith; praying five times a day; daily fasting during Ramadan; giving charity; and making a pilgrimage to Mecca. Many Muslims also observe dietary rules that forbid foods (like pork) and alcohol.

...

Muslims believe in a Day of Judgment, when righteous souls will go to heaven and wrongdoers will go to hell. Muslims see Islam as the final, complete, and correct revelation in the monotheistic tradition of the three faiths.[3]

Each Had A Founding Prophet!

Each of the three 'Abrahamic' religions had a *founding prophet* who provided a written record, establishing a framework of laws, customs and core values.

The writings of each religion's **founding prophets** are considered by their adherents to be **the definitive "Word of God," i.e. sacred, holy —** which *cannot be questioned!*

Moses was Judaism's founding prophet.   Attributed to him is **The Torah,** also known as the five books of Moses.

Saul of Tarsus, also known as The Apostle Paul, was Christianity's founding prophet.   His writings account for over half of the New Testament books. He is responsible for the main doctrines of Christianity.

Muhammad is known as Islam's founding prophet.   He is credited with establishing **The Quran,** upon which the religion of Islam is based.

[3]exploros,   'Three   Religions,   One   God,'   accessed   20   Jul   2025,
https://www.exploros.com/summary/Three-Religions-One-God

Christianity And Islam Do Not Sanction Criticism of Their Founders!

What differentiates the **Faith of Abraham,** found in the Torah of Moses, from its "offshoots," Christianity and Islam?

In Judaism, *we are allowed to criticize Moses and other prophets!* Yet, in Christianity and Islam, neither allows such.

In fact, Christianity and Islam actually *venerate their founding prophets (and saints, etc.) to a level of idolatry* which has well documented prohibitions found in the Torah of Moses![4]   There are, obviously, a multitude of examples of this in common media, so I'll not elaborate on that herein.

Again, in Judaism, we can criticize our prophets!   One example of Jewish criticism can be found in a commentary on Matos-Masei (Parashah reading in July 2025) by Project Genesis from Torah.org!

> In Parshas Mattos, HaShem tells Moshe, "achieve vengeance for the Children of Israel from the Midianites," but Moshe turns to Israel and tells them "to deliver the vengeance of G-d in Midyan" [Num. 31:2-3]. G-d says it is the vengeance of the Children of Israel, and Moshe says it is the vengeance of Hashem! How can Moshe tell Israel something so different than what he was told? ...[5]

Why Didn't Christianity And Islam Just Accept Judaism?

In a nutshell, so to speak, **I believe that Christianity and Islam**

---

[4]Some passages from The Pill Tanakh (Leningrad Codex based) relating to idolatry: Exodus 20:3-4; 22:19, Leviticus 19:4; 26:1, Deuteronomy 4:23; 17:1-5; 30:17-18, Judges 10:13-14, 1 Samuel 15:23, Isaiah 44:9-21; 45:20; 46:6-7; 48:5, 66:3, Jeremiah 2:11, Habakkuk 2:18-19, Psalms 16:4; 115:4-8; 135:15-18.

[5]Rabbi Yaakov Menken, 'Matos-Masei,' https://torah.org, accessed 25 July 2025, https://torah.org/parsha/matos,masei/

rejected the form of Judaism which had become a construct of the Talmud and the Oral Law, before and after it was codified, i.e. Talmudic/Rabbinic Judaism!

Such outsiders as Jewish Karaites, early gentile Christians and Islamists **rightly discerned** that Rabbinical Judaism did not represent their own religious yearnings and desires.

Long before the **degradation of the Jewish High Priesthood,** it is apparent that the Israelite nation **abandoned the Torah and Biblically based practices.**

Even at the time of King Asa, who reigned about 100 years after Israel's first king, Saul, **there is evidence that the nation had abandoned the Torah!**

15 3 Now for long seasons Israel was without the true God, and without a teaching priest, and without Torah; 12 And they entered into the covenant to seek Yehovah, the God of their fathers, with all their heart and with all their soul; 13 and that whosoever would not seek Yehovah, the God of Israel, should be put to death, whether small or great, whether man or woman.
[2 Chronicles 15:3, 12-13 The Pill Tanakh]

Is Karaism The True Expression of The Biblically Based Faith of Abraham?

History of Karaism

Karaism is the original Judaism which has existed throughout history under various names incl. Righteous, Sadducees, Boethusians, Ananites and Karaites, all of whom obeyed the Torah with no additions.

Karaism has been around since God gave his laws to the Jewish people. At first those who followed YHWH's laws were merely called "Righteous" and it was only in the 9th century CE that they came to be called Karaites. The question of why God's followers are today called Karaites is really a question of the origin of the other sects. At first there was no reason to label the righteous as a separate sect because there was only the one sect which consisted of the whole Jewish people. Throughout history a variety of sects appeared and it was only to distinguish the righteous from these other groups which caused them in different periods to take on such names as Sadducees, Boethusians, Ananites, and Karaites.

...

Then in the 8th century a last glimmer of hope appeared in the form of a shrewd leader named Anan ben David.   Anan organized various non-Talmudic groups and lobbied the Caliphate to establish a second Exilarchate for those who refused to live according to the Talmud's man-made laws. The Muslims granted Anan and his followers the religious freedom to practice Judaism in the way of their anscestors. Anan himself was not a Karaite; although Anan rejected the Talmud he used similar irrational methods of interpreting Scripture as the Rabbis, such as intentionally taking words out of context.   Anan's followers became known as *Ananites* and this group continued to exist down until the 10th century. On the other hand, those Jews who continued to practice the Tanach-based religion of their anscestors became known as *Bnei Mikra* ("Followers of Scripture") which was also abbreviated as *Karaim* ("Scripturalists"), in English "Karaites". This name derived from the old Hebrew word for the Hebrew Bible: *Mikra, Kara*. The name Karaim, meaning "Scripturalists", distinguished these Jews from the camp of the Rabbis who called themselves *Rabaniyin* ("Followers of the Rabbis") or *Talmudiyin* ("Followers of the Talmud").[6]

I have said elsewhere that I consider myself to be a Karaite, a

---

[6]The Karate Korner, `History of Karaism', accessed 5 Aug 2025, https://www.karaite-korner.org/history.shtml. To access, you may need to choose "History of Karaism" from the home page: https://www.karaite-korner.org/

Jewish Scripturalist!

Although I recognize contributions, especially to Jewish liturgy, from Talmudists–Rabbis, I disavow any recognition, authority or adherence to the Oral Law.

To me, the Jewish Scriptures, particularly the Tanakh[7] sourced from the ancient Hebrew–language based Leningrad Codex, is the basis for the authority in Jewish worship!

Moreover, I am of the opinion that Israelites (the Jewish people) can legitimately practice their religion without having a Temple in Yerushalam and without having a functioning High Priesthood!

If that statement is correct, then the multitude of Jewish Synagogues throughout the world *are actually practicing a legitimate form of religion*   just as much as Christian denominations and Muslim mosques!

Of course, that argument is counter to those who want to hold the Jewish people to Biblically subscribed rules and regulations regarding the High Preisthood as well as a standing Temple!   In so doing, those folks appear to try to justify their own religious traditions *replacing* that of the Jewish people.

Further, if those folks insist on holding the Israelite–Jewish people

---

[7]Tanakh. "Though the word "Bible" is commonly used by non-Jews -- as are the terms "Old Testament" and "New Testament" — the appropriate term to use for the Hebrew scriptures ("scripture" is a synonym used by both Jews and non-Jews) is Tanakh. This word is derived from the Hebrew letters of its three components:
Torah: The Books of Genesis (Bereshit), Exodus (Shemot), Leviticus (Vayikrah), Numbers (Bamidbar) and Deuteronomy (Devarim).
Nevi'im (Prophets): The Books of Joshua, Judges, I Samuel, II Samuel, I Kings, II Kings, Isaiah, Jeremiah, Ezekiel, Hosea, Joel, Amos, Obadiah, Jonah, Micah, Nahum, Habukkuk, Zephaniah, Haggai, Zechariah, and Malachi. (The last twelve are sometimes grouped together as "Trei Asar" ["Twelve"].)
Ketuvim (Writings): The Books of Psalms, Proverbs, Job, Song of Songs, Ruth, Lamentations, Ecclesiastes, Esther, Daniel (although not all that is included in the Christian Canon), Ezra and Nehemiah, I Chronicles, and II Chronicles."
Shamash Hadash, "The Tanakh," Jewish Virtual Library, accessed 25 April 2021, https://www.jewishvirtuallibrary.org/the-tanakh.

to those Biblically subscribed standards (Temple/High Priesthood), they must necessarily also remove the books of Daniel and Ezekiel and any other contemporary prophets from their Bibles because those prophets served during the time of the Babylonian exile when the Temple had been destroyed by Nebuchadnezzar and no defining High Priest was serving!

Rich Influence In Liturgical Forms

Talmudic/Rabbinic Judaism filled a void, but it was based mostly on the sayings of its sages, with a sprinkling of Biblical passages, often taken out of their natural contexts.

Although I might agree that Talmudic Judaism is not representative of a true **Biblically based religion** in practice, I would not want to minimize the contributions of the rabbis to current liturgical forms.

I realize I am biased, but I am very appreciative of the richness of Jewish worship tradition that has been handed down to the Jewish people in present forms of worship.

It is Talmudic Judaism which has provided those rich traditions to the Jewish people as a whole.

On a personal note, as a self–described Karaite, not only do I enjoy Sabbath and High Holiday liturgical tradition, but I also prefer the rabbinic passover ritual over the Karaite one. The Karaite passover service is primarily a recitation of Scripture, and although I appreciate and enjoy that, I find that rabbinic passover tradition, which is geared towards younger folks, to be a true joy!

Abraham, Ishmael, the Sabbath, etc.

I find it ironic that **neither Christianity nor Islam accepts the Torah of Moses as binding!** Yet, it appears that many ideas and knowledge of Abraham, Ishmael, the Sabbath, etc. no doubt would have come from **The Written Torah Of Moses!**

One particular and telling example is that neither Christianity nor

Islam regards the Torah command to keep **the seventh–day Sabbath** as either significant or important!

I would say that it is not just from an ethos of moral relativism and intellectual superiority as much as it is likely from a latent anti-Hebrew — anti-Jewish foundation. *"We know better!"* is the sense I deem as the basis for the rejection of the rules and regulations codified in The Torah of Moses.

Christians typically parrot the teaching of Paul from Romans 14 which essentially infers that ***any day is acceptable for observing the day of rest.*** Islam, has a "Jum'ah," which is their day of prayer and worship, **and they basically state that God does not rest, so they don't either.**

I want to emphasize that both positions in Christianity and Islam **contravene the clear teachings found in the Torah of Moses, especially relating to the seventh–day Sabbath!**

Changing The Sabbath
A Roman Catholic View of The Ten Commandments

Called also simply THE COMMANDMENTS, COMMANDMENTS OF GOD, or THE DECALOGUE (Gr. deka, ten, and logos, a word), the Ten Words of Sayings, the latter name generally applied by the Greek Fathers.

The Ten Commandments are precepts bearing on the fundamental obligations of religion and morality and embodying the revealed expression of the Creator's will in relation to man's whole duty to God and to his fellow-creatures. They are found twice recorded in the Pentateuch, in Exodus 20 and Deuteronomy 5, but are given in an abridged form in the catechisms. Written by the finger of God on two tables of stone, this Divine code was received from the Almighty by Moses amid the thunders of Mount Sinai, and by him made the ground-work of the

Mosaic Law. Christ resumed these Commandments in the double precept of charity--love of God and of the neighbour; He proclaimed them as binding under the New Law in Matthew 19 and in the Sermon on the Mount (Matthew 5). He also simplified or interpreted them, e.g. by declaring unnecessary oaths equally unlawful with false, by condemning hatred and calumny as well as murder, by enjoining even love of enemies, and by condemning indulgence of evil desires as fraught with the same malice as adultery (Matthew 5). The Church, on the other hand, after changing the day of rest from the Jewish Sabbath, or seventh day of the week, to the first, made the Third Commandment refer to Sunday as the day to be kept holy as the Lord's Day. The Council of Trent (Sess. VI, can. xix) condemns those who deny that the Ten Commandments are binding on Christians. ...[8]

The Church, on the other hand, after changing the day of rest from the Jewish Sabbath, or seventh day of the week, to the first, made the Third Commandment refer to Sunday as the day to be kept holy as the Lord's Day. The Council of Trent (Sess. VI, can. xix) condemns those who deny that the Ten Commandments are binding on Christians. ...

Ask A Muslim: Friday Sabbath

Why does the Islam religion not hold on to the creator's law of the Sabbath, but instead keep it on a Friday?

The only two days that are mentioned in the Quran

---

[8]Kevin Knight, 'The Ten Commandments', New Advent, accessed 16 Dec 2024, https://www.newadvent.org/cathen/04153a.htm.

are Friday and Saturday.   Friday is significant in Islam for a variety of reasons. This significance is established through the Quran and the Hadith (the sayings of the Prophet Muhammad pbuh). Chapter 62 of the Quran explains that Friday is a day to pray in congregation and offer gratitude to God for his blessings and leave all worldly matters. Once the obligation is made, then one can seek God's bounty.

"Believers! When the call to the prayer is made on the day of congregation (Friday), hurry towards the reminder of God and leave off your trading. That is better for you, if only you knew. Then, when the prayer has ended, disperse in the land and seek out God's bounty. Remember God often so that you may prosper." (Quran, Chapter 62:9-11)

Furthermore, as per Book 4 (Kitab Al-Salat) of Sahih Muslim, Hadith Number 1862:

"It is narrated by Abu Huraira and Huraira that the Messenger of Allah (may peace be upon him) said: It was Friday from which Allah diverted those who were before us. For the Jews (the day set aside for prayer) was Sabt (Saturday), and for the Christians it was Sunday. And Allah turned towards us and guided us to Friday (as the day of prayer) for us. In fact, He (Allah) made Friday, Saturday and Sunday (as days of prayer). In this order would they (Jews and Christians) come after us on the Day of Resurrection. We are the last of (the Ummahs) among the people in this world and the first among the created to be judged on the Day of Resurrection. In one narration it is: ', to be judged among them."

Another hadith of the Prophet Muhammad pbuh states that Friday was the day when Adam was created. This is the day when he entered paradise and was then expelled from it.

"Shabbat (שַׁבָּת ; related to Hebrew verb "cease, rest") is the seventh day of the Jewish week and is the day of rest and abstention from work as commanded by God," according to the Jewish Virtual Library. "Shabbat involves two interrelated commandments: to remember (zachor) and to observe (shamor)." Sabbath is considered a day to rest and abstain from work on the basis that God created heaven and earth and then rested on the seventh day. Islam acknowledges the six-part creation and Sabbath. However, it denies that the Creator needed rest. The story of the Sabbath breakers is mentioned in the seventh chapter of the Quran when the followers of Sabbath transgressed and greed took the place of rest.

"God: there is no god but Him, the Ever Living, the Ever Watchful. Neither slumber nor sleep overtakes him. All that is in the heavens and in the earth belongs to Him. Who is there that can intercede with Him except by His leave? He knows what is before them and what is behind them, but they do not comprehend any of His knowledge except what He wills. His throne extends over the heavens and the earth; it does not weary Him to preserve them both. He is the Most High, The Tremendous." (Quran, Chapter 2:255)

I have listed a few explanations of the significance of Friday in Islam, although there are more hadiths and verses that depict why it is considered blessed and holier than any other day of the week.

Disclaimer: I am not a religious scholar. I tried to answer these questions to the best of my knowledge and understanding of Islam as a Muslim. [9]

---

[9] Maimoona Harrington, 'Ask A Muslim: Friday Sabbath,' last modified 11 July 2021, https://favs.news/ask-a-muslim-friday-sabbath/

Sabbath is considered a day to rest and abstain from work on the basis that God created heaven and earth and then rested on the seventh day. Islam acknowledges the six-part creation and Sabbath. However, it denies that the Creator needed rest. The story of the Sabbath breakers is mentioned in the seventh chapter of the Quran when the followers of Sabbath transgressed and greed took the place of rest.

The Sabbath In Exodus 20

כ <u>ו</u> זָכוֹר֩ אֶת־י֨וֹם הַשַּׁבָּ֜ת לְקַדְּשׁ֗וֹ שֵׁ֤שֶׁת יָמִים֙
תַּֽעֲבֹד֙ וְעָשִׂ֣יתָ כָּל־מְלַאכְתֶּ֔ךָ וְיוֹם֙ הַשְּׁבִיעִ֔י שַׁבָּ֣ת
l לַֽיהוָ֖ה אֱלֹהֶ֑יךָ לֹֽא־תַעֲשֶׂ֣ה כָל־מְלָאכָ֡ה אַתָּ֣ה l
וּבִנְךָֽ־וּבִתֶּ֣ךָ עַבְדְּךָ֤ וַאֲמָֽתְךָ֙ וּבְהֶמְתֶּ֔ךָ וְגֵרְךָ֖ אֲשֶׁ֥ר
בִּשְׁעָרֶֽיךָ כִּ֣י שֵֽׁשֶׁת־יָמִים֩ עָשָׂ֨ה יְהוָ֜ה אֶת־הַשָּׁמַ֣יִם
וְאֶת־הָאָ֗רֶץ אֶת־הַיָּם֙ וְאֶת־כָּל־אֲשֶׁר־בָּ֔ם וַיָּ֖נַח
בַּיּ֣וֹם הַשְּׁבִיעִ֑י עַל־כֵּ֗ן בֵּרַ֧ךְ יְהוָ֛ה אֶת־י֥וֹם הַשַּׁבָּ֖ת
וַֽיְקַדְּשֵֽׁהוּ׃

20 <u>6</u> Remember the sabbath day, to keep it holy. Six days shalt thou labour, and do all thy work; but the seventh day is the sabbath unto Yehovah thy God, in it thou shalt not do any manner of work, thou, nor thy son, nor thy daughter, nor thy man-servant, nor thy maid-servant, nor thy cattle, nor thy stranger that is within thy gates; for in six days Yehovah made heaven and earth, the sea, and all that in them is, and rested on the seventh day; wherefore Yehovah blessed the sabbath day, and hallowed it.
[Exodus 20:6 The Pill Tanakh]

Three Religions – THREE Gods!

I have presented just a couple of views from Christianity and Islam regarding the Sabbath, but that in no way exhausts the subject.

Again, I consider the Hebrew–language based Jewish Scriptures based upon the ancient Leningrad Codex as authoritative. That is where I am coming from. However, it is evident to me that **Jesus is NOT** יְהוָה **[Yehovah] and Allah is NOT** יְהוָה **[Yehovah]!**

When יְהוָה *[Yehovah] said very clearly:*

זָכוֹר֙ אֶת־י֤וֹם הַשַּׁבָּת֙ לְקַדְּשׁ֔וֹ שֵׁ֣שֶׁת יָמִים֙ כ ו
תַּֽעֲבֹד֙ וְעָשִׂ֣יתָ כָּל־מְלַאכְתֶּ֔ךָ וְי֙וֹם֙ הַשְּׁבִיעִ֔י שַׁבָּ֣ת ׀
לַֽיהוָ֖ה אֱלֹהֶ֑יךָ לֹֽא־תַעֲשֶׂ֣ה כָל־מְלָאכָ֡ה

"Remember the sabbath day, to keep it holy. Six days shalt thou labour, and do all thy work; but the seventh day is the sabbath unto Yehovah thy God, in it thou shalt not do any manner of work,"

*He **distinguished** **Himself** **from** **all** **other** **Gods**!*

יְהוָה [Yehovah] did not allow the children of Israel to just interpret His words to mean something they do not mean!

Theirs was to hear and obey,   not to conclude that *any day could serve as Sabbath,*   including the first day of the week, Sunday, as most Christians have come to hold; *not to say that He does not rest because He is the creator,*   so we can pray and worship on Friday, as the Islamists do.

Keeping the seventh-day Sabbath is the acknowledgement and recognition that יְהוָה **[Yehovah] is the One True God, and there is no other!**

Acknowledging and recognizing any other day than the seventh day as Sabbath (or day of worship) **should be considered to be an expression of <u>worshipping</u> a <u>different</u> <u>God!</u>**

A simple example can be shown from the Christian Scriptures (New Testament) regarding **The Torah of Moses.**

> For verily I say unto you, Till heaven and earth pass, one jot or one tittle shall in no wise pass from the law, till all be fulfilled. [Matthew 5:18 KJV]

> And it is easier for heaven and earth to pass, than one tittle of the law to fail. [Luke 16:17 KJV]

In an apparent *contradiction* to the words of Jesus, Paul said:

> 5   One man esteemeth one day above another: another esteemeth every day alike. Let every man be fully persuaded in his own mind.
> 6   He that regardeth the day, regardeth it unto the Lord; and he that regardeth not the day, to the Lord he doth not regard it. He that eateth, eateth to the Lord, for he giveth God thanks; and he that eateth not, to the Lord he eateth not, and giveth God thanks. [Romans 14:5-6 KJV]

In my opinion, Christianity should not "Have it both ways!"

Either the words of Jesus, **which <u>appear</u> <u>to</u> <u>uphold</u> <u>the</u> <u>Torah</u> <u>of</u> Moses,** should be considered to be authoritative or the words of Paul, **who consistently misapplied the Torah and took it out of its natural context to change its intended audience and meaning,** [10] are representative of correct Christian Biblical authority!

Quite obviously, in practice, it is the words of Paul which are the authority in Christianity.

<u>Were</u> <u>it</u> <u>not</u> <u>so,</u> <u>obviously</u> <u>the</u> <u>words</u> <u>of</u> <u>Jesus</u> <u>would</u> <u>prevail</u>

---

[10] For more information on this subject, please refer to my book "Jesus Cannot Be The Jewish Messiah*" – Robert M. Pill, copyright © 2023.

<u>over</u> <u>those</u> <u>of</u> <u>Paul</u>!   As I stated earlier, Paul is Christianity's founding prophet; his writings are the source of its main doctrines.

Two Usurper Religions!

The two usurper religions, Christianity and Islam, claim the promises to the Israelite–Jewish people as their own!

Christians believe they are the seed of Abraham, not through the covenant of *physical* circumcision, but simply through their faith!

> **4** <u>11</u> And he received the sign of circumcision, a seal of the righteousness of the faith which he had yet being uncircumcised: that he might be the father of all them that believe, though they be not circumcised; that righteousness might be imputed unto them also:
>
> <u>12</u> And the father of circumcision to them who are not of the circumcision only, but who also walk in the steps of that faith of our father Abraham, which he had being yet uncircumcised.
>
> <u>13</u> For the promise, that he should be the heir of the world, was not to Abraham, or to his seed, through the law, but through the righteousness of faith.
>
> <u>14</u> For if they which are of the law be heirs, faith is made void, and the promise made of none effect:
>
> <u>15</u> Because the law worketh wrath: for where no law is, there is no transgression.
>
> <u>16</u> Therefore it is of faith, that it might be by grace; to the end the promise might be sure to all the seed; not to that only which is of the law, but to that also which is of the faith of Abraham; who is the father of us all,
>
> [Romans 4:11-16 KJV]

Muslims claim that the the ancient Jewish Scriptures were corrupted.   For example, instead of honoring the ancient Jewish Scripture, they want the Scriptures to say that it was **Ishmael, not Isaac,** that Abraham was asked to sacrifice on Mount Moriah.

According to the ancient Hebrew–language based Jewish Scriptures, both Ishmael and Abraham were circumcised on the same day.

יז כג וַיִּקַּח אַבְרָהָם אֶת־יִשְׁמָעֵאל בְּנוֹ וְאֵת
כָּל־יְלִידֵי בֵיתוֹ וְאֵת כָּל־מִקְנַת כַּסְפּוֹ כָּל־זָכָר
בְּאַנְשֵׁי בֵּית אַבְרָהָם וַיָּמָל אֶת־בְּשַׂר עָרְלָתָם
בְּעֶצֶם הַיּוֹם הַזֶּה כַּאֲשֶׁר דִּבֶּר אִתּוֹ אֱלֹהִים:

17 23 And Abraham took Ishmael his son, and all that were born in his house, and all that were bought with his money, every male among the men of Abraham's house, and circumcised the flesh of their foreskin in the selfsame day, as God had said unto him.

כד וְאַבְרָהָם בֶּן־תִּשְׁעִים וָתֵשַׁע שָׁנָה בְּהִמֹּלוֹ בְּשַׂר
עָרְלָתוֹ:

24 And Abraham was ninety years old and nine, when he was circumcised in the flesh of his foreskin.

כה וְיִשְׁמָעֵאל בְּנוֹ בֶּן־שְׁלֹשׁ עֶשְׂרֵה שָׁנָה בְּהִמֹּלוֹ
אֵת בְּשַׂר עָרְלָתוֹ:

25 And Ishmael his son was thirteen years old, when he was circumcised in the flesh of his foreskin.

כו בְּעֶצֶם הַיּוֹם הַזֶּה נִמּוֹל אַבְרָהָם וְיִשְׁמָעֵאל
בְּנוֹ:

26   In the selfsame day was Abraham

circumcised, and Ishmael his son.

כז וְכָל־אַנְשֵׁי בֵיתוֹ יְלִיד בָּיִת וּמִקְנַת־כֶּסֶף מֵאֵת
בֶּן־נֵכָר נִמֹּלוּ אִתּוֹ׃

27 And all the men of his house, those born in the house, and those bought with money of a foreigner, were circumcised with him.
[Genesis 17:23-27 The Pill Tanakh]

The covenant of circumcision between יְהֹוָה [Yehovah] and Abraham saw its first male child, Isaac, **who was the first son born of a circumcised father under that covenant.**

Notably, **Ishmael was conceived when Abraham was uncircumcised!**

Again, both **usurper religions** of **Christianity and Islam** interpret the Jewish Scriptures to be about themselves, *to the exclusion of the Israelite–Jewish people!*

Christianity and Islam both claim the covenant of circumcision to apply to themselves!

As a result, **neither acknowledges the exclusivity of the covenant of circumcision to the Israelite–Jewish people,** which came about *physically* through the first son, Isaac, who was the very first son conceived by circumcised Abraham under the covenant of circumcision.

The covenant of circumcision was passed down from father to son beginning with Abraham, Isaac and Jacob — the progenitors of the Israelite, Jewish people.

The covenant that יְהֹוָה [Yehovah] made exclusively with Abraham and his male descendants was for all time — Eternal and Everlasting!

Ancient Prophecy
Past, Future Or Double Fulfillment?

In our modern age it is probably not surprising that *relativism* has become a dominant force in culture as well as religious circles.

Ours is a time when the last century has given rise to personal automobiles for most households; flying in modern aircraft for the general populace has become routine; the rise of a movie industry has influenced the culture with dreams of psychic fantasy and moral corruption; common media, through newspapers, television and the internet have brought just–in–time news to a population that previously got news often days or weeks after occurrence.

Previous populations, before the industrial revolution began in Great Britain in the 1700's and in the United States in the 1800's, had a much more innocent outlook no doubt associated with a much slower pace in everyday living and outside news gathering.

There is an ancient prophecy near the end of the book of Daniel which many have interpreted to be about our time in history.

many shall run to and fro,
and knowledge shall be increased

יב **א** וּבָעֵת הַהִיא יַעֲמֹד מִיכָאֵל הַשַּׂר הַגָּדוֹל
הָעֹמֵד עַל־בְּנֵי עַמֶּךָ וְהָיְתָה עֵת צָרָה אֲשֶׁר
לֹא־נִהְיְתָה מִהְיוֹת גּוֹי עַד הָעֵת הַהִיא וּבָעֵת
הַהִיא יִמָּלֵט עַמְּךָ כָּל־הַנִּמְצָא כָּתוּב בַּסֵּפֶר׃

12 1 And at that time shall Michael stand up, the great prince who standeth for the children of thy people; and there shall be a time of trouble, such as never was since there was a nation even to that same time; and at that time thy people shall be delivered, every one that shall be found written in the book.

ב רַבִּים מִיְּשֵׁנֵי אַדְמַת־עָפָר יָקִיצוּ אֵלֶּה לְחַיֵּי
עוֹלָם וְאֵלֶּה לַחֲרָפוֹת לְדִרְאוֹן עוֹלָם:

2 And many of them that sleep in the dust of the earth shall awake, some to everlasting life, and some to reproaches and everlasting abhorrence

ג וְהַמַּשְׂכִּלִים יַזְהִרוּ כְּזֹהַר הָרָקִיעַ וּמַצְדִּיקֵי
הָרַבִּים כַּכּוֹכָבִים לְעוֹלָם וָעֶד:

3 And they that are wise shall shine as the brightness of the firmament; and they that turn the many to righteousness as the stars for ever and ever.

ד וְאַתָּה דָנִיֵּאל סְתֹם הַדְּבָרִים וַחֲתֹם הַסֵּפֶר
עַד־עֵת קֵץ יְשֹׁטְטוּ רַבִּים וְתִרְבֶּה הַדָּעַת:

4 But thou, O Daniel, shut up the words, and seal the book, even to the time of the end; many shall run to and fro, and knowledge shall be increased.' [Daniel 9:1-4 The Pill Tanakh]

12 3 And they that are wise shall shine as the brightness of the firmament; and they that turn the many to righteousness as the stars for ever and ever.

4 But thou, O Daniel, shut up the words, and seal the book, even to the time of the end; many shall run to and fro, and knowledge shall be increased.' [Daniel 12:3-4 The Pill Tanakh]

and they that turn the many to righteousness ...

Daniel 12:3 is often overshadowed by verse 4, *"... and knowledge shall be increased."* However, the idea of **turning many to righteousness** is compelling especially since it is a theme of much of the prophetic statements throughout Daniel.

7 18 But the saints of the Most High shall receive the kingdom, and possess the kingdom for ever, even for ever and ever. [Dariel 7:18 The Pill Tanakh]

12 10 Many shall purify themselves, and make themselves white, and be refined; but the wicked shall do wickedly; and none of the wicked shall understand; but they that are wise shall understand.
[Daniel 12:10 The Pill Tanakh]

Ancient Prophecy
Past, Future Or Double Fulfillment?

Have *all* ancient prophecies been fulfilled? Are any of them for a future time? Can ancient prophecy have multiple fulfillments?

I believe it is obvious that Daniel 12:4, where it states, "and knowledge shall be increased" may not have been evidently fulfilled until our modern age.

There are some (found prominently in the Christian community) who hold to the idea of multiple (dual/double) fulfillments of ancient prophecies.[1]   Often, they are consumed with prophetic fulfillment.

---

[1] A double fulfillment or dual fulfillment of a Bible prophecy is the circumstance in which the prophecy has both a short-term and long-term fulfillment. A prophecy is made, and the first

An example of this is an interpretation of Ezekiel 37:3 "... can these bones live?" Many hold that to be fulfilled on May 14, 1948 when Israel officially became a modern nation.

Can These Bones Live?

לֹז ‫ג‬ וַיֹּאמֶר אֵלַי בֶּן־אָדָם הֲתִחְיֶינָה הָעֲצָמוֹת
הָאֵלֶּה וָאֹמַר אֲדֹנָי יְהוִה אַתָּה יָדָעְתָּ׃

37 ‫3‬ And He said unto me: 'Son of man, can these bones live?' And I answered: 'O Lord GOD [Adonai Yehovi], Thou knowest.'

In Ezekiel, chapter 37, Ezekiel speaks about **"Can these bones live?"** Later in that chapter his prophesy talks about **joining two sticks,** of Israel and Judah, **into one stick.**

It should be noted that עֵץ is most often translated as **"tree or wood",** and seldom, if ever, as **"stick!":**

---

fulfillment comes to pass relatively soon thereafter. Later, there is a second fulfillment to the prophecy, and that second fulfillment is usually fuller and more literal. So, there is a "near" fulfillment and a "far" fulfillment. A prophecy having a dual fulfillment helps to unify Scripture and emphasizes God's masterful control of events. There are several examples of prophecies with a double fulfillment.

Joel's Holy Spirit Prophecy

The prophet Joel, speaking of the day of the Lord, said, "And afterward, I will pour out my Spirit on all people. Your sons and daughters will prophesy, your old men will dream dreams, your young men will see visions. Even on my servants, both men and women, I will pour out my Spirit in those days" (Joel 2:28–29). The first fulfillment of this prophecy is when Peter stood up on the day of Pentecost and spoke the same words to those gathered in Jerusalem (Acts 2:14–18). Indeed, miraculous manifestations of God's power through the Holy Spirit happened on that day (Acts 2:1–13). However, that was only a partial fulfillment of Joel's prophecy. The prophecy goes on to speak of "blood and fire and billows of smoke" (Joel 2:30), astronomical signs (verse 31), and the gathering of all nations for judgment (Joel 3:1–2). None of that has yet happened; therefore, the ultimate fulfillment of Joel 2 awaits Jesus' second coming. At that time, God's enemies will experience "the great and dreadful day of the Lord" (Joel 2:31; cf. Revelation 16:14–16). ...

Got Questions, 'What does it mean that a prophecy has a double/dual fulfillment', gotquestions.org, accessed Sep 18 2025, https://www.gotquestions.org/prophecy-double-dual-fulfillment.html

לֹז יט‎ דַּבֵּר אֲלֵהֶם כֹּה־אָמַר֮ אֲדֹנָי יְהוִֹה֒ הִנֵּה אֲנִי לֹקֵחַ
אֶת־עֵץ יוֹסֵף֮ אֲשֶׁר בְּיַד־אֶפְרַיִם וְשִׁבְטֵי יִשְׂרָאֵל חֲבֵרָיו֒[2]
וְנָתַתִּי אוֹתָם עָלָיו אֶת־עֵץ יְהוּדָה וַעֲשִׂיתִם לְעֵץ אֶחָד וְהָיוּ
אֶחָד בְּיָדִי:

37 19 say into them: Thus saith the Lord GOD
[Adonai Yehovi]: Behold, I will take the stick of
Joseph, which is in the hand of Ephraim, and the
tribes of Israel his companions; and I will put them
unto him together with the stick of Judah, and make
them one stick, and they shall be one in My hand.

Unfortunately, often modern groups want to reserve for
themselves that these prophecies are about them, rather than the
actual Jewish people to whom the prophecy was given!

QUESTION

What is the meaning of the Valley of Dry Bones in Ezekiel 37?

ANSWER

Ezekiel's vision of the valley of dry bones (Ezekiel
37:1–14) came to him after God had directed him to
prophesy the rebirth of Israel in chapter 36. God
announced, through the prophet, that Israel will be
restored to her land in blessing under the leadership
of "David, My servant [who] shall be king over them"
(Ezekiel 37:24), clearly a reference to the future
under Jesus Christ the Messiah, descendant of
David (Isaiah 7:14; 9:6–7; Luke 1:31–33). However,
this promise seemed impossible in light of Israel's
present condition. She was "dead" as a nation,
deprived of her land, her king, and her temple. She
had been divided and dispersed for so long that

unification and restoration seemed impossible. So
God gave Ezekiel the vision of the dry bones as
sign.[3]

**"... clearly a reference to the future under Jesus Christ
the Messiah, descendant of David (Isaiah 7:14; 9:6–7;
Luke 1:31–33)."**

Perhaps it is the result of Christianity embracing the idea that
"They are descendants of Abraham by faith," to which many
interpret to actually mean that <u>they</u> <u>alone</u> are the **"Israel of God,"**
which gives authority for their claim of *replacing* the natural
descendants of Abraham, Isaac and Jacob!

**As such, they take the Jewish Scriptures to be exclusively
about themselves, rather than the real descendants of Israel!**

Another example of how Christian apologists want to reserve
ancient texts as confirmation for their beliefs is found in their
interpretation of Jeremiah 31:31ff.

Retired professor Uri Yosef has an excellent analysis, the end
summary of which I will quote with its reference:

Jeremiah 31:30-36 [31-37]

Will The Real "New Covenant" Please Stand Up!

V. Summary
The analysis presented in this essay demonstrates
that the correct reading and interpretation of
Jeremiah 31:30-36 [31-37] refutes the claims made
by Christian missionaries, and exposes the

---

[3]GotQuestions.org, 'What Is The Meaning Of The Valley Of Dry Bones In Ezekiel 37,' accessed
26 Sep 2025, https://www.gotquestions.org/valley-dry-bones.html

attempted revision by author of the Epistle to the Hebrews of Jeremiah's prophetic message concerning the eternity of the Jewish people and the Torah and turn it into a prophecy about the advent of Jesus and Christianity's New Testament.

Throughout the Hebrew Bible prophets foretell that, in the messianic era, the Jewish people will be observing the commandments of the Torah:

> **Isaiah 2:3 - And many people shall go and say, "Come, and let us go up to the mountain of the Lord, to the House of the God of Jacob, and He will teach us of His ways, and we will walk in His paths;" for out of Zion shall Torah emerge, and the word of the Lord from Jerusalem.**

> **Ezekiel 37:24 - And My servant David shall be king over them, and one shepherd shall shall be for them all; and they shall follow My ordinances, and observe My statutes, and perform them.**

> **Malachi 3:22 [4:4] - Remember the Torah of Moses My servant; that which I commanded him in Horeb for all Israel, statutes and ordinances.**

It is evident that Jeremiah's use of the term בְּרִית חֲדָשָׁה, a new covenant, does not involve the replacement of the (eternal) Torah by the New

Testament. Rather, it signals a renewal of the original Sinai Covenant, which was declared to be everlasting, through its placement within us along with סֵפֶר הַבְּרִית, the Book of the Covenant, to make them an inseparable part of the Jewish way of life. The term בְּרִית חֲדָשָׁה would be meaningless in any context other than one that describes the revitalized original Sinai Covenant, along with the Torah, which cannot be replaced, superseded, or rescinded.[4]

The term בְּרִית חֲדָשָׁה would be meaningless in any context other than one that describes the revitalized original Sinai Covenant, along with the Torah, which cannot be replaced, superseded, or rescinded.

Where Are We In Biblical History?[5]

Is there a prophecy in the Jewish Scriptures that might inform us as to what point in Biblical history we are in?

It appears that there is a chapter in the book of Hosea that may express our time in history!

גֿ א וַיֹּאמֶר יְהוָה אֵלַי עוֹד לֵךְ אֱהַב־אִשָּׁה אֲהֻבַת
רֵעַ וּמְנָאָפֶת כְּאַהֲבַת יְהוָה אֶת־בְּנֵי יִשְׂרָאֵל וְהֵם
פֹּנִים אֶל־אֱלֹהִים אֲחֵרִים וְאֹהֲבֵי אֲשִׁישֵׁי עֲנָבִים׃

3 **1** And Yehovah said unto me: 'Go yet, love a woman beloved of her friend and an

---

[4]Uri Yosef, 'Will The Real '' New Covenant'' Please Stand Up!{Jeremiah 31:30-36 [31-37]} ', accessed 20 Jan 2018, https://uriyosef.wordpress.com/2020/03/19/will-the-real-new-covenant-please-stand-up-2/

[5]I want to emphasize the relevance of Hosea 3. Also, I should note that I had an email dialogue from a response to my website (https://the-iconoclast.org) where the person wanted to try to convince me that Judaism is not relevant without a High Priest and a Temple in his effort to try to prove that Christianity is the only true religion!

adulteress, even as Yehovah loveth the children of Israel, though they turn unto other gods, and love cakes of raisins.

בּ וָאֶכְּרֶהָ לִּי בַּחֲמִשָּׁה עָשָׂר כָּסֶף וְחֹמֶר שְׂעֹרִים
וְלֵתֶךְ שְׂעֹרִים:

2 So I bought her to me for fifteen pieces of silver and a homer of barley, and a half-homer of barley;

גּ וָאֹמַר אֵלֶיהָ יָמִים רַבִּים תֵּשְׁבִי לִי לָא תִזְנִי וְלָא
תִהְיִי לְאִישׁ וְגַם־אֲנִי אֵלָיִךְ:

3 and I said unto her: 'Thou shalt sit solitary for me many days; thou shalt not play the harlot, and thou shalt not be any man's wife; nor will I be thine.'

דּ כִּי ׀ יָמִים רַבִּים יֵשְׁבוּ בְּנֵי יִשְׂרָאֵל אֵין מֶלֶךְ וְאֵין
שָׂר וְאֵין זֶבַח וְאֵין מַצֵּבָה וְאֵין אֵפוֹד וּתְרָפִים:

4 For the children of Israel shall sit solitary many days without king, and without prince, and without sacrifice, and without pillar, and without ephod or teraphim;

הּ אַחַר יָשֻׁבוּ בְּנֵי יִשְׂרָאֵל וּבִקְשׁוּ אֶת־יְהוָה
אֱלֹהֵיהֶם וְאֵת דָּוִד מַלְכָּם וּפָחֲדוּ אֶל־יְהוָה
וְאֶל־טוּבוֹ בְּאַחֲרִית הַיָּמִים:

5 afterward shall the children of Israel return, and seek Yehovah their God, and David their king; and shall come trembling unto Yehovah and to His goodness in the end of days.
[Hosea 3:1-5 The Pill Tanakh]

---

4 For the children of Israel shall sit solitary many days without king, and

without prince, and without sacrifice, and without pillar, and without ephod or teraphim;

5 afterward shall the children of Israel return, and seek Yehovah their God, and David their king; and shall come trembling unto Yehovah and to His goodness in the end of days.
[Hosea 3:4-5 The Pill Tanakh]

Are we living in such a time?

Actually, I am not quite sure! Hosea prophesied about one hundred years before Nebuchadnezzar conquered Judah and destroyed the Temple in יְרוּשָׁלַם Yerushalam. Surely, during the time the children of Israel were in Babylon, it was such a time when there was no king, prince, sacrifice, etc. No doubt but Hosea could have been directly speaking about that time, _**and not about our time several thousands of years removed**_!

A Prophet Like Moses

יח יח נָבִיא אָקִים לָהֶם מִקֶּרֶב אֲחֵיהֶם כָּמוֹךָ וְנָתַתִּי דְבָרַי בְּפִיו וְדִבֶּר אֲלֵיהֶם אֵת כָּל־אֲשֶׁר אֲצַוֶּנּוּ:

18 18 I will raise them up a prophet from among their brethren, like unto thee; and I will put My words in his mouth, and he shall speak unto them all that I shall command him.

יט וְהָיָה הָאִישׁ אֲשֶׁר לֹא־יִשְׁמַע אֶל־דְּבָרַי אֲשֶׁר יְדַבֵּר בִּשְׁמִי אָנֹכִי אֶדְרֹשׁ מֵעִמּוֹ:

19 And it shall come to pass, that whosoever will not hearken unto My words which he

shall speak in My name, I will require it of him. [Deuteronomy 18:18-19 The Pill Tanakh]

Deuteronomy 18:18-19 records *"I will raise them up a prophet from among their brethren, like unto thee; and I will put My words in his mouth, and he shall speak unto them all that I shall command him."*

Within Islam, commentators have associated *"brethren"* to infer and mean *a son of Abraham!* Thus, they claim that Muhammad, as a *"brethren,"* fulfilled the prophecy in Deuteronomy 18, *"I will raise them up a prophet from among their brethren,..."*

I believe it is unfortunate that an outlook of *relativism* has also pervaded Islamic thought! Earlier, I presented the *exclusive* nature of the covenant between יְהֹוָה [Yehovah] and Abraham came through Isaac, the first son born of circumcised father, Abraham, under that covenant of circumcision!

Obviously, <u>Ishmael</u> <u>was</u> <u>not</u> <u>that</u> <u>son</u>, as although his father was Abraham, he was circumcised on the same day as Abraham his father, when he was thirteen years old! Thus, Muhammad did not come from an Abrahamic family line originating through that exclusive covenant of circumcision between יְהֹוָה [Yehovah] and Abraham!

The Prophetic Link as the Brethren of the Israelites

Ishmael and Isaac were both brothers and they were the children of Prophet Abraham. When Prophet Moses, may peace and blessings be upon him, was quoting God as promising to send a prophet like Moses the verse says *'from among their brethren'.* Who are the brethren of the Israelites? They are, simply, the Ishmaelites. This is a clear and straightforward indication that the prophet who is going to be 'like unto Moses' from the brethren of the Israelites is Prophet

Muhammad, may peace and blessing be upon him.

In fact, the Hebrew dictionary of the Bible defines brethren, as used in the biblical sense, in the following terms: it says it is the personification of a group of tribes who were regarded as near kinsmen to the Israelites. There is no nearer kinsmen tribe to the Israelites other than the Ishmaelites because they are their brethren- descendents of the brother of Isaac. It is consistent.

Moses and Muhammad: "Like Unto Thee"

I think perhaps one crucial phrase that is used in the verse is when it says "from among their brethren, like unto thee." (Duet 18:18) God is saying that He will raise up a prophet that is similar to Moses. This is significant because the only great prophets, who came after Moses, were Jesus and Muhammad. However, it does not apply to Jesus because he is not really from the brethren of the Israelites. He is himself an Israelite.[6]

There are many articles relating to this topic that can be found on Islamic themed websites. I use the above quote as one reference, but it is my understanding that much of Islam supports the idea that Muhammad is the fulfillment of the prophetic discourse in Deuteronomy 18 regarding *"I will raise them up a prophet from among their brethren, like unto thee; and I will put My words in his mouth, and he shall speak unto them all that I shall command him."*

In spite of Islamic belief that Muhammad was among *Moses's*

---

[6] Dr. Jamal Badawi, from transcribed audio lectures on www.jamalbadawi.org, 'Muhammad: A Prophet Like Unto Moses,' accessed 28 Sep 2025, https://www.whyislam.org/muhammad-a-prophet-like-unto-moses/

brethren, he could not be considered to be **a brother to Moses under the covenant of circumcision coming directly out of the line of Abraham, Isaac and Jacob,** as was Moses and the Israelite people.

Coincidentally, the Christian religion also wants to reserve to themselves the fulfillment of Deuteronomy 18:18-19!

17 And now, brethren, I wot that through ignorance ye did it, as did also your rulers.

18 But those things, which God before had shewed by the mouth of all his prophets, that Christ should suffer, he hath so fulfilled.

19 Repent ye therefore, and be converted, that your sins may be blotted out, when the times of refreshing shall come from the presence of the Lord;

20 And he shall send Jesus Christ, which before was preached unto you:

21 Whom the heaven must receive until the times of restitution of all things, which God hath spoken by the mouth of all his holy prophets since the world began.

22 For Moses truly said unto the fathers, A prophet shall the Lord your God raise up unto you of your brethren, like unto me; him shall ye hear in all things whatsoever he shall say unto you.

23 And it shall come to pass, that every soul, which will not hear that prophet, shall be destroyed from among the people.

24 Yea, and all the prophets from Samuel and those that follow after, as many as have spoken, have likewise foretold of these days.

25 Ye are the children of the prophets, and of the covenant which God made with our fathers, saying unto Abraham, And in thy seed shall all the kindreds of the earth be blessed.

26 Unto you first God, having raised up his

Son Jesus, sent him to bless you, in turning away every one of you from his iniquities.
[Acts 3:17-26 KJV]

Christianity's book of Acts also uses the Jewish Scriptures to justify their beliefs, reserving to themselves the exclusive fulfillment of for the ancient prophecies!

But, what do the Jewish Scriptures say regarding the fulfillment of the prophecy, *"I will raise them up a prophet from among their brethren, like unto thee;"* ?

כז יה וַיְדַבֵּר מֹשֶׁה אֶל־יְהוָה לֵאמֹר:

27 15 And Moses spoke unto Yehovah, saying:

יז יִפְקֹד יְהוָה אֱלֹהֵי הָרוּחֹת לְכָל־בָּשָׂר אִישׁ עַל־הָעֵדָה:

16 'Let Yehovah, the God of the spirits of all flesh, set a man over the congregation,

יז אֲשֶׁר־יֵצֵא לִפְנֵיהֶם וַאֲשֶׁר יָבֹא לִפְנֵיהֶם וַאֲשֶׁר יוֹצִיאֵם וַאֲשֶׁר יְבִיאֵם וְלֹא תִהְיֶה עֲדַת יְהוָה כַּצֹּאן אֲשֶׁר אֵין־לָהֶם רֹעֶה:

17 who may go out before them, and who may come in before them, and who may lead them out, and who may bring them in; that the congregation of Yehovah be not as sheep which have no shepherd.'

יח וַיֹּאמֶר יְהוָה אֶל־מֹשֶׁה קַח־לְךָ אֶת־יְהוֹשֻׁעַ בִּן־נוּן אִישׁ אֲשֶׁר־רוּחַ בּוֹ וְסָמַכְתָּ אֶת־יָדְךָ עָלָיו:

18 And Yehovah said unto Moses: 'Take thee Joshua the son of Nun, a man in whom is spirit, and lay thy hand upon him;

יט וְהַעֲמַדְתָּ אֹתוֹ לִפְנֵי אֶלְעָזָר הַכֹּהֵן וְלִפְנֵי
כָּל־הָעֵדָה וְצִוִּיתָה אֹתוֹ לְעֵינֵיהֶם:

19 and set him before Eleazar the priest, and before all the congregation; and give him a charge in their sight.

כ וְנָתַתָּה מֵהוֹדְךָ עָלָיו לְמַעַן יִשְׁמְעוּ כָּל־עֲדַת
בְּנֵי יִשְׂרָאֵל:

20 And thou shalt put of thy honour upon him, that all the congregation of the children of Israel may hearken.

כא וְלִפְנֵי אֶלְעָזָר הַכֹּהֵן יַעֲמֹד וְשָׁאַל לוֹ בְּמִשְׁפַּט
הָאוּרִים לִפְנֵי יְהוָה עַל־פִּיו יֵצְאוּ וְעַל־פִּיו יָבֹאוּ
הוּא וְכָל־בְּנֵי־יִשְׂרָאֵל אִתּוֹ וְכָל־הָעֵדָה:

21 And he shall stand before Eleazar the priest, who shall inquire for him by the judgment of the Urim before Yehovah; at his word shall they go out, and at his word they shall come in, both he, and all the children of Israel with him, even all the congregation.'
[Numbers 27:15-21 The Pill Tanakh]

18 And Yehovah said unto Moses: 'Take thee Joshua the son of Nun, a man in whom is spirit, and lay thy hand upon him;

...

21 And he shall stand before Eleazar the priest, who shall inquire for him by the judgment of the Urim before Yehovah; at his word shall they go out, and at his word they shall come in, both he, and all the children of Israel with him, even all the congregation.'

Numbers 27, found in The Torah of Moses, clearly shows who יְהֹוָה [Yehovah] intended to fulfill the prophecy *"I will raise them up a prophet from among their brethren, like unto thee;"* — to be יְהוֹשֻׁעַ בִּן־נוּן Joshua the son of Nun!

A question might reasonably be asked, **"Since both Islam and Christianity use the Jewish Scriptures to affirm their beliefs, why don't they also refer to Numbers 27 to acknowledge that Joshua was the intended person to fulfill the prophecy declared in Deuteronomy 18?"**

An obvious answer might be, **"Because in doing so, it would mean that they would have to acquiesce to, and acknowledge the Jewish Scriptures as authoritative!"**

Moreover, fully exploring the 'whole counsel of Scripture' would necessarily discredit the Christian and Islamic *practice of using selective quotes from the Jewish Scriptures* to justify their interpretations and core beliefs!

Head of Gold

בֹ לֹא אַנְתָּה מַלְכָּא חָזֵה הֲוַיְתָ וַאֲלוּ צְלֵם חַד
שַׂגִּיא צַלְמָא דִּכֵּן רַב וְזִיוֵהּ יַתִּיר קָאֵם לְקָבְלָךְ
וְרֵוֵהּ דְּחִיל:

2 31 Thou, O king, sawest, and behold a
great image. This image, which was mighty,
and whose brightness was surpassing, stood
before thee; and the appearance thereof was
terrible.

לֹב הוּא צַלְמָא רֵאשֵׁהּ דִּי־דְהַב טָב חֲדֹוֹהִי
וּדְרָעֹוֹהִי דִּי כְסַף מְעֹוֹהִי וְיַרְכָתֵהּ דִּי נְחָשׁ:

32 As for that image, its head was of fine gold,
its breast and its arms of silver, its belly and its
thighs of brass,

לֹג שָׁקֹוֹהִי דִּי פַרְזֶל רַגְלֹוֹהִי מִנְּהֵין[1] דִּי פַרְזֶל
וּמִנְּהֵין[2] דִּי חֲסַף:

33 its legs of iron, its feet part of iron and part
of clay.

לֹד חָזֵה הֲוַיְתָ עַד דִּי הִתְגְּזֶרֶת אֶבֶן דִּי־לָא
בִידַיִן וּמְחָת לְצַלְמָא עַל־רַגְלֹוֹהִי דִּי פַרְזְלָא
וְחַסְפָּא וְהַדֵּקֶת הִמּוֹן:

34 Thou sawest till that a stone was cut out
without hands, which smote the image upon
its feet that were of iron and clay, and broke
them to pieces.

לֹה בֵּאדַיִן דָּקוּ כַחֲדָה פַּרְזְלָא חַסְפָּא נְחָשָׁא
כַסְפָּא וְדַהֲבָא וַהֲוֹוֹ כְּעוּר מִן־אִדְּרֵי־קַיְט וּנְשָׂא

מִנְּהֹון[1]
וּמִנְּהֹון[2]

הֵמּוֹן֙ רוּחָ֔א וְכָל־אֲתַ֖ר לָא־הִשְׁתֲּכַ֣ח לְה֑וֹן וְאַבְנָ֣א
‏ דִּי־מְחָ֣ת לְצַלְמָ֗א הֲוָ֞ת לְט֤וּר רַב֙ וּמְלָ֖ת
כָּל־אַרְעָֽא׃

35 Then was the iron, the clay, the brass, the silver, and the gold, broken in pieces together, and became like the chaff of the summer threshing-floors; and the wind carried them away, so that no place was found for them; and the stone that smote the image became a great mountain, and filled the whole earth.

לוּ   דְּנָ֣ה חֶלְמָ֔א וּפִשְׁרֵ֥הּ נֵאמַ֖ר קֳדָם־מַלְכָּֽא׃

36 This is the dream; and we will tell the interpretation thereof before the king.

לז   אַ֣נְתְּה מַלְכָּ֔א מֶ֖לֶךְ מַלְכַיָּ֑א דִּ֚י אֱלָ֣הּ שְׁמַיָּ֔א
מַלְכוּתָ֥א חִסְנָ֛א וְתָקְפָּ֥א וִיקָרָ֖א יְהַב־לָֽךְ׃

37 Thou, O king, king of kings, unto whom the God of heaven hath given the kingdom, the power, and the strength, and the glory;

לח   וּבְכָל־דִּ֣י דָֽיְרִ֣ין ³   בְּנֵי־אֲנָשָׁ֞א חֵיוַ֤ת בָּרָא֙
וְעוֹף־שְׁמַיָּא֙ יְהַ֣ב בִּידָ֔ךְ וְהַשְׁלְטָ֖ךְ בְּכָלְּה֑וֹן
אַנְתְּה־ה֔וּא רֵאשָׁ֖ה דִּ֥י דַהֲבָֽא׃

38 and wheresoever the children of men, the beasts of the field, and the fowls of the heaven dwell, hath He given them into thy hand, and hath made thee to rule over them all; thou art the head of gold.

לט   וּבָתְרָ֗ךְ תְּק֤וּם מַלְכ֣וּ אָחֳרִ֔י אֲרַ֖עא מִנָּ֑ךְ

דָּאֲרִין ³

וּמַלְכוּ תְלִיתָאָה⁴ אָחֳרִי דִּי נְחָשָׁא דִּי תִשְׁלַט
בְּכָל־אַרְעָא׃

__39__ And after thee shall arise another kingdom inferior to thee; and another third kingdom of brass, which shall bear rule over all the earth.

מ וּמַלְכוּ רְבִיעָאָה⁵ תֶּהֱוֵא תַקִּיפָה כְּפַרְזְלָא
כָּל־קֳבֵל דִּי פַרְזְלָא מְהַדֵּק וְחָשֵׁל כֹּלָּא
וּכְפַרְזְלָא דִּי־מְרָעַע כָּל־אִלֵּין תַּדִּק וְתֵרֹעַ׃

__40__ And the fourth kingdom shall be strong as iron; forasmuch as iron breaketh in pieces and beateth down all things; and as iron that crusheth all these, shall it break in pieces and crush.

מא וְדִי־חֲזַיְתָה רַגְלַיָּא וְאֶצְבְּעָתָא מִנְּהֵן⁶ חֲסַף
דִּי־פֶחָר וּמִנְּהֵין⁷ פַּרְזֶל מַלְכוּ פְלִיגָה תֶּהֱוֵה
וּמִן־נִצְבְּתָא דִי פַרְזְלָא לֶהֱוֵא־בַהּ כָּל־קֳבֵל דִּי
חֲזַיְתָה פַּרְזְלָא מְעָרַב בַּחֲסַף טִינָא׃

__41__ And whereas thou sawest the feet and toes, part of potters' clay, and part of iron, it shall be a divided kingdom; but there shall be in it of the firmness of the iron, forasmuch as thou sawest the iron mixed with miry clay.

מב וְאֶצְבְּעָת רַגְלַיָּא מִנְּהֵין⁸ פַּרְזֶל וּמִנְּהֵין⁹
חֲסַף מִן־קְצָת מַלְכוּתָא תֶּהֱוֵה תַקִּיפָה וּמִנַּהּ
תֶּהֱוֵה תְבִירָה׃

__42__ And as the toes of the feet were part of iron,

---

⁴תְלִיתִיָא
⁵רְבִיעִיָה
⁶מִנְּהוֹן
⁷וּמִנְּהוֹן
⁸מִנְּהוֹן
⁹וּמִנְּהוֹן

and part of clay, so part of the kingdom shall
be strong, and part thereof broken.

מג וְדִי־¹⁰ חֲזַיִת פַּרְזְלָא מְעָרַב בַּחֲסַף טִינָא
מִתְעָרְבִין לֶהֱוֹן בִּזְרַע אֲנָשָׁא וְלָא־לֶהֱוֹן דָּבְקִין
דְּנָה עִם־דְּנָה הֵא־כְדִי פַרְזְלָא לָא מִתְעָרַב
עִם־חַסְפָּא:

43 And whereas thou sawest the iron mixed
with miry clay, they shall mingle themselves
by the seed of men; but they shall not cleave
one to another, even as iron doth not mingle
with clay.

מד וּבְיוֹמֵיהוֹן דִּי מַלְכַיָּא אִנּוּן יְקִים אֱלָהּ שְׁמַיָּא
מַלְכוּ דִּי לְעָלְמִין לָא תִתְחַבַּל וּמַלְכוּתָה לְעַם
אָחֳרָן לָא תִשְׁתְּבִק תַּדִּק וְתָסֵיף כָּל־אִלֵּין
מַלְכְוָתָא וְהִיא תְּקוּם לְעָלְמַיָּא:

44 And in the days of those kings shall the
God of heaven set up a kingdom, which shall
never be destroyed; nor shall the kingdom be
left to another people; it shall break in pieces
and consume all these kingdoms, but it shall
stand for ever.

מה כָּל־קֳבֵל דִּי־חֲזַיְתָ דִּי מִטּוּרָא אִתְגְּזֶרֶת אֶבֶן
דִּי־לָא בִידַיִן וְהַדֵּקֶת פַּרְזְלָא נְחָשָׁא חַסְפָּא
כַּסְפָּא וְדַהֲבָא אֱלָהּ רַב הוֹדַע לְמַלְכָּא מָה דִּי
לֶהֱוֵא אַחֲרֵי דְּנָה וְיַצִּיב חֶלְמָא וּמְהֵימַן פִּשְׁרֵהּ:

45 Forasmuch as thou sawest that a stone
was cut out of the mountain without hands,
and that it broke in pieces the iron, the brass,
the clay, the silver, and the gold; the great
God hath made known to the king what shall

come to pass hereafter; and the dream is
certain, and the interpretation thereof sure.
[Daniel 2:31-45 The Pill Tanakh]

**Nebuchadnezzar's dream from Daniel 2 revealed four
kingdoms.**   The first kingdom was Babylon, represented as **the
head of gold (Nebuchadnezzar).**

Similar visions or dreams of **the four kingdoms** are found in
Daniel 7 and 8. The angel Gabriel declares to Daniel the **second
and third kingdoms** in Chapter 8.

ח   יה   וַיְהִי בִּרְאֹתִי אֲנִי דָנִיֵּאל אֶת־הֶחָזֹון
וָאֲבַקְשָׁה בִינָה וְהִנֵּה עֹמֵד לְנֶגְדִּי כְּמַרְאֵה־גָבֶר׃

8 15 And it came to pass, when I, even I
Daniel, had seen the vision, that I sought to
understand it; and, behold, there stood
before me as the appearance of a man.

יו   וָאֶשְׁמַע קֹול־אָדָם בֵּין אוּלָי וַיִּקְרָא וַיֹּאמַר
גַּבְרִיאֵל הָבֵן לְהַלָּז אֶת־הַמַּרְאֶה׃

16 And I heard the voice of a man between the
banks of Ulai, who called, and said: 'Gabriel,
make this man to understand the vision.'

יז   וַיָּבֹא אֵצֶל עָמְדִי וּבְבֹאֹו נִבְעַתִּי וָאֶפְּלָה עַל־פָּנָי
וַיֹּאמֶר אֵלַי הָבֵן בֶּן־אָדָם כִּי לְעֶת־קֵץ הֶחָזֹון׃

17 So he came near where I stood; and when
he came, I was terrified, and fell upon my face;
but he said unto me: 'Understand, O son of
man; for the vision belongeth to the time of
the end.'

יח   וּבְדַבְּרֹו עִמִּי נִרְדַּמְתִּי עַל־פָּנַי אָרְצָה וַיִּגַּע־בִּי
וַיַּעֲמִידֵנִי עַל־עָמְדִי׃

18 Now as he was speaking with me, I fell into

a deep sleep with my face toward the ground; but he touched me, and set me upright.

יט וַיֹּאמֶר הִנְנִי מוֹדִיעֲךָ אֵת אֲשֶׁר־יִהְיֶה בְּאַחֲרִית הַזָּעַם כִּי לְמוֹעֵד קֵץ:

19 And he said: 'Behold, I will make thee know what shall be in the latter time of the indignation; for it belongeth to the appointed time of the end.

כ הָאַיִל אֲשֶׁר־רָאִיתָ בַּעַל הַקְּרָנָיִם מַלְכֵי מָדַי וּפָרָס:

20 The ram which thou sawest having the two horns, they are the kings of Media and Persia.

כא וְהַצָּפִיר הַשָּׂעִיר מֶלֶךְ יָוָן וְהַקֶּרֶן הַגְּדוֹלָה אֲשֶׁר בֵּין־עֵינָיו הוּא הַמֶּלֶךְ הָרִאשׁוֹן:

21 And the rough he-goat is the king of Greece; and the great horn that is between his eyes is the first king.
[Daniel 8:15-21 The Pill Tanakh]

19 And he said: 'Behold, I will make thee know what shall be in the latter time of the indignation; for it belongeth to the appointed time of the end.
20 The ram which thou sawest having the two horns, they are the kings of Media and Persia.
21 And the rough he-goat is the king of Greece; and the great horn that is between his eyes is the first king.
[Daniel 8:19-21 The Pill Tanakh]

The fourth kingdom (beast) is found in Chapter 7. Its name is not given. However, because we are now several thousand years removed from those prophecies, it is clear that the fourth kingdom was the Roman Empire continued in the Roman Catholic Church!

ז יה אֶתְכְּרִיַּת רוּחִי אֲנָה דָנִיֵּאל בְּגוֹא נִדְנֶה וְחֶזְוֵי רֵאשִׁי יְבַהֲלֻנַּנִי:

7 15 As for me Daniel, my spirit was pained in the midst of my body, and the visions of my head affrighted me.

יו קִרְבֵת עַל־חַד מִן־קָאֲמַיָּא וְיַצִּיבָא אֶבְעֵא־מִנֵּהּ עַל־כָּל־דְּנָה וַאֲמַר־לִי וּפְשַׁר מִלַּיָּא יְהוֹדְעִנַּנִי:

16 I came near unto one of them that stood by, and asked him the truth concerning all this. So he told me, and made me know the interpretation of the things:

יז אִלֵּין חֵיוָתָא רַבְרְבָתָא דִּי אִנִּין אַרְבַּע אַרְבְּעָה מַלְכִין יְקוּמוּן מִן־אַרְעָא:

17 These great beasts, which are four, are four kings, that shall arise out of the earth.

יח וִיקַבְּלוּן מַלְכוּתָא קַדִּישֵׁי עֶלְיוֹנִין וְיַחְסְנוּן מַלְכוּתָא עַד־עָלְמָא וְעַד עָלַם עָלְמַיָּא:

18 But the saints of the Most High shall receive the kingdom, and possess the kingdom for ever, even for ever and ever.'

יט אֱדַיִן צְבִית לְיַצָּבָא עַל־חֵיוְתָא רְבִיעָיְתָא דִּי־הֲוָת שָׁנְיָה מִן־כָּלְּהֵין[11] דְּחִילָה יַתִּירָה שְׁנַּהּ[12] דִּי־פַרְזֶל וְטִפְרַיַהּ דִּי־נְחָשׁ אָכְלָה מַדֲּקָה וּשְׁאָרָא בְּרַגְלַיהּ רָפְסָה:

כלהון[11]
שניה[12]

<u>19</u> Then I desired to know the truth concerning the fourth beast, which was diverse from all of them, exceeding terrible, whose teeth were of iron, and its nails of brass; which devoured, brake in pieces, and stamped the residue with its feet;

כ וְעַל־קַרְנַיָּא עֲשַׂר דִּי בְרֵאשַׁהּ וְאָחֳרִי דִּי סִלְקַת
וּנְפַלָה[13] מִן־קֳדָמַהּ[14] תְּלָת וְקַרְנָא דִכֵּן וְעַיְנִין
לַהּ וְפֻם מְמַלִּל רַבְרְבָן וְחֶזְוַהּ רַב מִן־חַבְרָתַהּ׃

<u>20</u>   and concerning the ten horns that were on its head, and the other horn which came up, and before which three fell; even that horn that had eyes, and a mouth that spoke great things, whose appearance was greater than that of its fellows.

כא   חָזֵה הֲוֵית וְקַרְנָא דִכֵּן עָבְדָה קְרָב
עִם־קַדִּישִׁין וְיָכְלָה לְהוֹן׃

<u>21</u> I beheld, and the same horn made war with the saints, and prevailed against them;

כב עַד דִּי־אֲתָה עַתִּיק יוֹמַיָּא וְדִינָא יְהִב לְקַדִּישֵׁי
עֶלְיוֹנִין וְזִמְנָא מְטָה וּמַלְכוּתָא הֶחֱסִנוּ קַדִּישִׁין׃

<u>22</u>   until the Ancient of days came, and judgment was given for the saints of the Most High; and the time came, and the saints possessed the kingdom.

כג כֵּן אֲמַר חֵיוְתָא רְבִיעָיְתָא מַלְכוּ רְבִיעָאָה[15]
תֶּהֱוֵא בְאַרְעָא דִּי תִשְׁנֵא מִן־כָּל־מַלְכְוָתָא וְתֵאכֻל
כָּל־אַרְעָא וּתְדוּשִׁנַּהּ וְתַדְּקִנַּהּ׃

<u>13</u>וּנְפַלוּ
<u>14</u>קֳדָמַיהּ
<u>15</u>רְבִיעָיָא

23 Thus he said: 'The fourth beast shall be a fourth kingdom upon earth, which shall be diverse from all the kingdoms, and shall devour the whole earth, and shall tread it down, and break it in pieces.

כד וְקַרְנַיָּא עֲשַׂר מִנַּהּ מַלְכוּתָה עַשְׂרָה מַלְכִין יְקֻמוּן וְאָחֳרָן יְקוּם אַחֲרֵיהוֹן וְהוּא יִשְׁנֵא מִן־קַדְמָיֵא וּתְלָתָה מַלְכִין יְהַשְׁפִּל:

24   And as for the ten horns, out of this kingdom shall ten kings arise; and another shall arise after them; and he shall be diverse from the former, and he shall put down three kings.

כה וּמִלִּין לְצַד עִלָּאָה[16] יְמַלִּל וּלְקַדִּישֵׁי עֶלְיוֹנִין יְבַלֵּא וְיִסְבַּר לְהַשְׁנָיָה זִמְנִין וְדָת וְיִתְיַהֲבוּן בִּידֵהּ עַד־עִדָּן וְעִדָּנִין וּפְלַג עִדָּן:

25   And he shall speak words against the Most High, and shall wear out the saints of the Most High; and he shall think to change the seasons and the law; and they shall be given into his hand until a time and times and half a time.

כו וְדִינָא יִתִּב וְשָׁלְטָנֵהּ יְהַעְדּוֹן לְהַשְׁמָדָה וּלְהוֹבָדָה עַד־סוֹפָא:

26   But the judgment shall sit, and his dominions shall be taken away, to be consumed and to be destroy unto the end.

כז וּמַלְכוּתָה וְשָׁלְטָנָא וּרְבוּתָא דִּי מַלְכְוָת תְּחוֹת כָּל־שְׁמַיָּא יְהִיבַת לְעַם קַדִּישֵׁי עֶלְיוֹנִין מַלְכוּתֵהּ

עֶלְיָא[16]

מַלְכוּת עָלַם וְכֹל שָׁלְטָנַיָּא לֵהּ יִפְלְחוּן
וְיִשְׁתַּמְּעוּן:

27 And the kingdom and the dominion, and
the greatness of the kingdoms under the
whole heaven, shall be given to the people of
the saints of the Most High; their kingdom is
an everlasting kingdom, and all dominions
shall serve and obey them.'

כח עַד־כָּה סוֹפָא דִי־מִלְתָא אֲנָה דָנִיֵּאל שַׂגִּיא ׀
רַעְיוֹנַי יְבַהֲלֻנַּנִי וְזִיוַי יִשְׁתַּנּוֹן עֲלַי וּמִלְּתָא בְּלִבִּי
נִטְרֵת:

28 Here is the end of the matter. As for me
Daniel, my thoughts much affrighted me, and
my countenance was changed in me; but I
kept the matter in my heart.
[Daniel 7:15-28 The Pill Tanakh]

**23 Thus he said: 'The fourth beast
shall be a fourth kingdom upon
earth, which shall be diverse from all
the kingdoms, and shall devour the
whole earth, and shall tread it down,
and break it in pieces.**

Within three chapters in Daniel, Chapter 2, 7 and 8, it appears that
**through Daniel we are presented a prediction of the
Kingdoms ruling the world to the time of the coming of a new
world represented by righteousness (declared at the end of
Chapter 2 and Chapter 7)!**

**45 Forasmuch as thou sawest that a
stone was cut out of the mountain
without hands, and that it broke in
pieces the iron, the brass, the clay,**

the silver, and the gold; the great God hath made known to the king what shall come to pass hereafter; and the dream is certain, and the interpretation thereof sure.

[Daniel 2:45 The Pill Tanakh]

קִרְבֵת עַל־חַד מִן־קָאֲמַיָּא וְיַצִּיבָא יז ז
אֶבְעֵא־מִנֵּהּ עַל־כָּל־דְּנָה וַאֲמַר־לִי וּפְשַׁר מִלַּיָּא
יְהוֹדְעִנַּנִי:

7 16 I came near unto one of them that stood by, and asked him the truth concerning all this. So he told me, and made me know the interpretation of the things:

אִלֵּין חֵיוָתָא רַבְרְבָתָא דִּי אִנִּין אַרְבַּע אַרְבְּעָה יז
מַלְכִין יְקוּמוּן מִן־אַרְעָא:

17 'These great beasts, which are four, are four kings, that shall arise out of the earth.

וִיקַבְּלוּן מַלְכוּתָא קַדִּישֵׁי עֶלְיוֹנִין וְיַחְסְנוּן יח
מַלְכוּתָא עַד־עָלְמָא וְעַד עָלַם עָלְמַיָּא:

18 But the saints of the Most High shall receive the kingdom, and possess the kingdom for ever, even for ever and ever.

[Daniel 7:16-18 The Pill Tanakh]

18 But the saints of the Most High shall receive the kingdom, and possess the kingdom for ever, even for ever and ever.

Summary

In Daniel 2, Nebuchadnezzar's dream is interpreted to declare that there would be four prominent kingdoms, essentially **"to the end of the age!"**

Following **'The Head of Gold'** — Babylon, the last three kingdoms, represented by **silver, bronze and iron,** are found in Chapters 7 and 8.

Just as the end of Chapter 2 declares

<u>45</u> Forasmuch as thou sawest that a stone was cut out of the mountain without hands, and that it broke in pieces the iron, the brass, the clay, the silver, and the gold; the great God hath made known to the king what shall come to pass hereafter; and the dream is certain, and the interpretation thereof sure.

A supernatural event will destroy the rulership of the four kingdoms and usher in the age of righteousness, represented by But the וִיקַבְּלוּן מַלְכוּתָא קַדִּישֵׁי עֶלְיוֹנִין וְיַחְסְנוּן מַלְכוּתָא קַדִּישֵׁי holy ones [saints] shall receive the kingdom,...!

יח   וִיקַבְּלוּן מַלְכוּתָא קַדִּישֵׁי עֶלְיוֹנִין

וְיַחְסְנוּן מַלְכוּתָא עַד־עָלְמָא וְעַד עָלַם

עָלְמַיָּא׃

<u>18</u> But the saints of the Most High shall receive the kingdom, and possess the kingdom for ever, even for ever and ever. [Daniel 7:18 The Pill Tanakh]

Judges, Kings, Prophets

The nation of Israel was established under a foundation of laws, statutes and ordinances along with the office of the Cohen Gadol, the High Priest. Nonetheless, **the nation was never under the exclusive authority of the High Priest.** From its very beginnings, Israel had Judges, followed by Kings and Prophets to help lead the nation.

To help provide understanding of Judges, Kings and Prophets are tables showing dates and times of their authority in ancient Israel.

A note on Hebrew transliteration in the following tables

I have tried to represent **a phonetic Hebrew pronunciation** using a method of transliteration that is entirely my own. It is based upon my understanding of the Hebrew vowel system used by the Masoretes from the Leningrad Codex[1] and codified by Ernest Klein.[2]

For example, for the sound of the Hebrew letter Ayin, with a kamatz vowel underneath (that looks like a 'T' with a short stem and pronounced with an emphatic 'AH'), as found in (עָ), I may use 'Ah' or 'Au.' The guttural Ayin ע sound is produced in the throat!

For the letter Alef with a patach underneath (אַ) I may use 'Uh' or 'o' as in (אַבְרָהָם) (Abraham), transliterated 'Uv'rah'hahm' or

---

[1] Let us say on the outset that the Leningrad Codex is one of the most important Hebrew documents extant, with ramifications and influence that is immeasurable. It is -- along with the other famous biblical codex, the Aleppo Codex -- one of the sources for biblical tradition, for the study of Hebrew Scriptures, and for providing an accurate text for the reading and writing of the Torah and the other books of the Bible.

The Leningrad Codex is the oldest complete manuscript of the Tanakh, the 39 books of the Bible. Written in Cairo on parchment in the year 1009 (the date appears on the manuscript), it is inextricably bound up with the Aleppo Codex, which is about a century older but undated. Moreover, the Aleppo Codex, housed for many years in the Aleppo Synagogue in Syria, was badly damaged in a fire during anti-Jewish riots in Syria in 1947, and so it is incomplete. The Aleppo Codex, now safely stored at the National Hebrew Library in Jerusalem, along with the Leningrad Codex, set the standard for the correct text of the Tanakh, including its vocalization and the musical accents (trop or te'amim) that accompany every word. Although the spelling of a word may be consistent in Hebrew, in the absence of vocalization (more commonly called the vowel "dots"), there can be variations as to how the letters are pronounced. Curt Leviant, 'Jewish Holy Scriptures: The Leningrad Codex', Jewish Virtual Library, accessed 13 Dec 2020, https://www.jewishvirtuallibrary.org/the-leningrad-codex.

[2] Ernest Klein, 'Transliteration Rules,' ''A Comprehensive Etymological Dictionary of the Hebrew Language For Readers of English'' (Carta, Jerusalem), Copyright © 1987 by The Beatrice & Author Minden Foundation & The University of Haifa, (pp. X I-XIII).

'Ov'rah'hahm.' The **patach,** which looks like an underline, is a *short vowel* and has the sound of *a* in *far* or as an *a* in *was.*

Many people want to pronounce the name 'Abraham' in a phonetic transliterated Hebrew with a sharp 'Ahv' sound as in 'Ahv'rah'hahm,' but it is better expressed as I've noted above with a short 'Uhv' sound at the beginning, since the *patach* underneath the Alef is *a short vowel.* For a better understanding of the sounds in the ancient Hebrew, please consider consulting appropriate sources![3]

Judges

Please note that the column named "Years" connotes _Years of Rest_, as in the Hebrew phrase וַתִּשְׁקֹט הָאָרֶץ אַרְבָּעִים שָׁנָה – **And the land had rest forty years.**

Judge	Years	Reference
עָתְנִיאֵל Ahth'nee'ail (Othniel)	40	Judges 3:9-11 And when the children of Israel cried unto Yehovah, Yehovah raised up a saviour to the children of Israel, who saved them, even Othniel the son of Kenaz, Caleb's younger brother. And the spirit of Yehovah came upon him, and he judged Israel; and he went out to war, and Yehovah delivered Cushan-rishathaim king of Aram into his hand; and his hand prevailed against Cushan-rishathaim. And the land had rest forty years. And Othniel the son of Kenaz died.

Continued on next page

---

[3]Such as a reputable Hebrew–English Dictionary, or my website (https://www.the-iconoclast.org/reference/HebrewLettersVowelsAccents.php), or in the chapter "Seek Yehovah" in my book 'Ad Mashiach Nagid - The Messiah in Daniel 9,' pp. 88-94; that chapter is also included in this book (with minor changes) due to its relevance!

Judge	Years	Reference
אֵהוּד Ei'huud (Ehud)	80	Judges 3:14-15, 30 And the children of Israel served Eglon the king of Moab eighteen years. But when the children of Israel cried unto Yehovah, Yehovah raised them up a saviour, Ehud the son of Gera, the Benjamite, a man left-handed; and the children of Israel sent a present by him unto Eglon the king of Moab. So Moab was subdued that day under the hand of Israel. And the land had rest eighty years.
שַׁמְגַּר Shuhm'guhr (Shamgar)		Judges 3:31 And after him was Shamgar the son of Anath, who smote of the Philistines six hundred men with an ox-goad; and he also saved Israel.
דְּבוֹרָה D'voh'rah (Deborah)		Judges 4:4-6 Now Deborah, a prophetess, the wife of Lappidoth, she judged Israel at that time. And she sat under the palm-tree of Deborah between Ramah and Beth-el in the hill-country of Ephraim; and the children of Israel came up to her for judgment. And she sent and called Barak the son of Abinoam out of Kedesh-naphtali, and said unto him: 'Hath not Yehovah, the God of Israel, commanded, saying: Go and draw toward mount Tabor, and take with thee ten thousand men of the children of Naphtali and of the children of Zebulun?

Continued on next page

Judge	Years	Reference
גִּדְעוֹן Geed'ohn (Gideon)	40	Judges 6:11, 14, 8:28 And the angel of Yehovah came, and sat under the terebinth which was in Ophrah, that belonged unto Joash the Abiezrite; and his son Gideon was beating out wheat in the winepress, to hide it from the Midianites. And the angel of Yehovah came, and sat under the terebinth which was in Ophrah, that belonged unto Joash the Abiezrite; and his son Gideon was beating out wheat in the winepress, to hide it from the Midianites. So Midian was subdued before the children of Israel, and they lifted up their heads no more. And the land had rest forty years in the days of Gideon.
יִפְתָּח Yeeph'takh (Jepthah)	6	Judges 11:1-5, 12:7 Now Jephthah the Gileadite was a mighty man of valour, and he was the son of a harlot; and Gilead begot Jephthah. And Gilead's wife bore him sons; and when his wife's sons grew up, they drove out Jephthah, and said unto him: 'Thou shalt not inherit in our father's house; for thou art the son of another woman.' Then Jephthah fled from his brethren, and dwelt in the land of Tob; and there were gathered vain fellows to Jephthah, and they went out with him. And it came to pass after a while, that the children of Ammon made war against Israel. And it was so, that when the children of Ammon made war against Israel, the elders of Gilead went to fetch Jephthah out of the land of Tob. And Jephthah judged Israel six years. Then died Jephthah the Gileadite, and was buried in one of the cities of Gilead.

Continued on next page

Judge	Years	Reference
אִבְצָן Eev'tzahn (Ibzan)	7	Judges 12:7-9 And Jephthah judged Israel six years. Then died Jephthah the Gileadite, and was buried in one of the cities of Gilead. And after him Ibzan of Beth-lehem judged Israel. And he had thirty sons, and thirty daughters he sent abroad, and thirty daughters he brought in from abroad for his sons. And he judged Israel seven years.
אֵילוֹן Ei'loan (Elon)	10	Judges 12:10-11 and Ibzan died, and was buried at Beth-lehem. And after him Elon the Zebulunite judged Israel; and he judged Israel ten years.
עַבְדּוֹן Uv'doan (Abdon)	8	Judges 12:12-14 And Elon the Zebulunite died, and was buried in Aijalon in the land of Zebulun. And after him Abdon the son of Hillel the Pirathonite judged Israel. And he had forty sons and thirty sons' sons, that rode on seventy ass colts; and he judged Israel eight years.
שִׁמְשׁוֹן Sheem'shoan (Samson)	20	Judges 13:24, 16:30-31 And the woman bore a son, and called his name Samson; and the child grew, and Yehovah blessed him. And Samson said: 'Let me die with the Philistines.' And he bent with all his might; and the house fell upon the lords, and upon all the people that were therein. So the dead that he slew at his death were more than they that he slew in his life. Then his brethren and all the house of his father came down, and took him, and brought him up, and buried him between Zorah and Eshtaol in the burying-place of Manoah his father. And he judged Israel twenty years.

Continued on next page

Judge	Years	Reference
עֵלִי Ei'lee (Eli)	40	1 Samuel 1:9, 4:18 So Hannah rose up after they had eaten in Shiloh, and after they had drunk--now Eli the priest sat upon his seat by the door-post of the temple of Yehovah; And it came to pass, when he made mention of the ark of God, that he fell from off his seat backward by the side of the gate, and his neck broke, and he died; for he was an old man, and heavy. And he had judged Israel forty years.

Continued on next page

Judge	Years	Reference
שְׁמוּאֵל Shmu'eil (Samuel)	All his life	1 Samuel 1:20, 26-28, 3:1, 7:15, 8:5, 9:27, 10:1 And it came to pass, when the time was come about, that Hannah conceived, and bore a son; and she called his name Samuel: 'because I have asked him of Yehovah.' And she said: 'Oh, my lord, as thy soul liveth, my lord, I am the woman that stood by thee here, praying unto Yehovah. For this child I prayed; and Yehovah hath granted me my petition which I asked of Him; therefore I also have lent him to Yehovah; as long as he liveth he is lent to Yehovah.' And he worshipped Yehovah there. And the child Samuel ministered unto Yehovah before Eli. And the word of Yehovah was precious in those days; there was no frequent vision. And Samuel judged Israel all the days of his life. And they said unto him: 'Behold, thou art old, and thy sons walk not in thy ways; now make us a king to judge us like all the nations.' As they were going down at the end of the city, Samuel said to Saul: 'Bid the servant pass on before us--and he passed on--but stand thou still at this time, that I may cause thee to hear the word of God.' Then Samuel took the vial of oil, and poured it upon his head, and kissed him, and said: 'Is it not that Yehovah hath anointed thee to be prince over His inheritance?

Continued on next page

Judge	Years	Reference
שְׁמוּאֵל Shmu'eil (Samuel)	All his life	1 Samuel 16:11-13, 19:18, 24:16-20 And Samuel said unto Jesse: 'Are here all thy children?' And he said: 'There remaineth yet the youngest, and, behold, he keepeth the sheep.' And Samuel said unto Jesse: 'Send and fetch him; for we will not sit down till he come hither.' And he sent, and brought him in. Now he was ruddy, and withal of beautiful eyes, and goodly to look upon. And Yehovah said: 'Arise, anoint him; for this is he.' Then Samuel took the horn of oil, and anointed him in the midst of his brethren; and the spirit of Yehovah came mightily upon David from that day forward. So Samuel rose up, and went to Ramah. Now David fled, and escaped, and came to Samuel to Ramah, and told him all that Saul had done to him. And he and Samuel went and dwelt in Naioth. And it came to pass, when David had made an end of speaking these words unto Saul, that Saul said: 'Is this thy voice, my son David?' And Saul lifted up his voice, and wept. And he said to David: 'Thou art more righteous than I; for thou hast rendered unto me good, whereas I have rendered unto thee evil. And thou hast declared this day how that thou hast dealt well with me; forasmuch as when Yehovah had delivered me up into thy hand, thou didst not kill me. For if a man find his enemy, will he let him go well away? wherefore Yehovah reward thee good for that which thou hast done unto me this day. And now, behold, I know that thou shalt surely be king, and that the kingdom of Israel shall be established in thy hand.

Continued on next page

Judge	Years	Reference
שְׁמוּאֵל Shmu'eil (Samuel)	All his life	1 Samuel 24:21-22, 25:1 Swear now therefore unto me by Yehovah, that thou wilt not cut off my seed after me, and that thou wilt not destroy my name out of my father's house.' And David swore unto Saul. And Saul went home; but David and his men got them up unto the stronghold. And Samuel died; and all Israel gathered themselves together, and lamented him, and buried him in his house at Ramah. And David arose, and went down to the wilderness of Paran.

Israel's Kings (Judah and Israel)

The following table shows the kings of Judah and Israel until the burning of Yerushalam. The column heading *"Years"* connotes the length of reign, which is presented mostly in years but sometimes days and/or months.

The year 1063 BCE is used as the beginning of Saul's reign. The number is just a guess, based upon the generally accepted year of the destruction of Yerushalam by Nebuchadnezzar of around 586 BCE. Using the amount of time recorded in the Jewish Scriptures, and working backwards to King Saul is how the dates have been determined. Again, the year under *"BCE"* is just a guess to approximate the beginning year of each king's reign.

Please note that the column *"BCE"* is not exactly chronological. **The kings of Judah are used as the baseline time** and the column *"Reference"* shows the reign of each king based upon the timeline of a king of Judah or Israel with the passage(s) in the Jewish Scriptures where the information is found.

Judah	Israel	Years	BCE	Reference
	שָׁאוּל Shah'uul (Saul)	2	1063	1 Samuel 13:1 Saul was ---- years old when he began to reign; and two years he reigned over Israel.
	אִישׁ־בֹּשֶׁת Eesh-boh'sheth (Ish-bosheth)	2	1061	(At the Start of David's Reign in Hebron) 2 Samuel 2:10 Ish-bosheth Saul's son was forty years old when he began to reign over Israel, and he reigned two years. But the house of Judah followed David.

Continued on next page

Judah	Israel	Years	BCE	Reference
דָּוִד Dah'veed (David)		40	1061	2 Samuel 2:11 And the time that David was king in Hebron over the house of Judah was seven years and six months. 2 Samuel 5:4 David was thirty years old when he began to reign, and he reigned forty years.
שְׁלֹמֹה Shlo'mo (Solomon)		40	1021	1 Kings 11:42-43 And the time that Solomon reigned in Yerushalam over all Israel was forty years. And Solomon slept with his fathers, and was buried in the city of David his father; and Rehoboam his son reigned in his stead.
רְחַבְעָם R'khav'ahm (Rehoboam)		17	981	1 Kings 14:21 And Rehoboam the son of Solomon reigned in Judah. Rehoboam was forty and one years old when he began to reign, and he reigned seventeen years in Yerushalam, the city which Yehovah had chosen out of all the tribes of Israel, to put His name there; and his mother's name was Naamah the Ammonitess.
	יָרְבְעָם Y'rahv'ahm (Jeroboam)	22	981	1 Kings 14:20 And the days which Jeroboam reigned were two and twenty years; and he slept with his fathers, and Nadab his son reigned in his stead.

Continued on next page

Judah	Israel	Years	BCE	Reference
אֲבִיָּם Uh'vee'yahm (Abijam)		3	964	1 Kings 15:1-2 Now in the eighteenth year of king Jeroboam the son of Nebat began Abijam to reign over Judah. Three years reigned he in Yerushalam; and his mother's name was Maacah the daughter of Abishalom.
אָסָא Ah'sah (Asa)		41	961	1 Kings 15:8-10 And Abijam slept with his fathers; and they buried him in the city of David; and Asa his son reigned in his stead. And in the twentieth year of Jeroboam king of Israel began Asa to reign over Judah. And forty and one years reigned he in Yerushalam; and his mother's name was Maacah the daughter of Abishalom.
	נָדָב Nah'dahv (Nadab)	2	920	1 Kings 15:25 And Nadab the son of Jeroboam began to reign over Israel in the second year of Asa king of Judah, and he reigned over Israel two years.
	בַּעְשָׁא Buhuh'shah (Baasa)	24	918	1 Kings 15:33 In the third year of Asa king of Judah began Baasa the son of Ahijah to reign over all Israel in Tirzah, and reigned twenty and four years.
	אֵלָה Ei'lah (Elah)	2	894	1 Kings 16:8 In the twenty and sixth year of Asa king of Judah began Elah the son of Baasa to reign over Israel in Tirzah, and reigned two years.

Continued on next page

Judah	Israel	Years	BCE	Reference
	זִמְרִי Zeem'ree (Zimri)	7 Days	892	1 Kings 16:15 In the twenty and seventh year of Asa king of Judah did Zimri reign seven days in Tirzah. Now the people were encamped against Gibbethon, which belonged to the Philistines.
	עָמְרִי Ahm'ree (Omri)	12	892	1 Kings 16:23-24 In the thirty and first year of Asa king of Judah began Omri to reign over Israel, and reigned twelve years; six years reigned he in Tirzah. *And he bought the hill Samaria of Shemer for two talents of silver; and he built on the hill, **and called the name of the city which he built, after the name of Shemer, the owner of the hill, Samaria.***
	אַחְאָב Uhkh'ahv (Ahab)	22	880	1 Kings 16:29 And in the thirty and eighth year of Asa king of Judah began Ahab the son of Omri to reign over Israel; and Ahab the son of Omri reigned over Israel in Samaria twenty and two years.
יְהוֹשָׁפָט Y'ho'shah'phat (Jehoshaphat)		25	920	1 Kings 22:41-42 And Jehoshaphat the son of Asa began to reign over Judah in the fourth year of Ahab king of Israel. Jehoshaphat was thirty and five years old when he began to reign; and he reigned twenty and five years in Yerushalam. And his mother's name was Azubah the daughter of Shilhi.

Continued on next page

Judah	Israel	Years	BCE	Reference
	אֲחַזְיָהוּ Uh'khaz'yahu (Ahaziah)	2	858	1 Kings 22:52 Ahaziah the son of Ahab began to reign over Israel in Samaria in the seventeenth year of Jehoshaphat king of Judah, and he reigned two years over Israel.
	יְהוֹרָם Y'ho'rahm (Jehoram)	12	856	2 Kings 3:1 Now Jehoram the son of Ahab began to reign over Israel in Samaria in the eighteenth year of Jehoshaphat king of Judah, and reigned twelve years.
יְהוֹרָם Y'ho'rahm (Jehoram)		8	895	2 Kings 8:16-17 And in the fifth year of Joram the son of Ahab king of Israel, Jehoshaphat being the king of Judah, Jehoram the son of Jehoshaphat king of Judah began to reign. Thirty and two years old was he when he began to reign; and he reigned eight years in Yerushalam.
אֲחַזְיָהוּ Uh'khuz'yah'hu (Ahaziah)		1	887	2 Kings 8:25-26 In the twelfth year of Joram the son of Ahab king of Israel did Ahaziah the son of Jehoram king of Judah begin to reign. Two and twenty years old was Ahaziah when he began to reign; and he reigned one year in Yerushalam. And his mother's name was Athaliah the daughter of Omri king of Israel.
	יֵהוּא Yei'hu (Jehu)	28	844	2 Kings 10:36 And the time that Jehu reigned over Israel in Samaria was twenty and eight years.

Continued on next page

Judah	Israel	Years	BCE	Reference
עֲתַלְיָה Uh'thuhl'yah (Athaliah)		7	886	2 Kings 11:1-4 Now when Athaliah the mother of Ahaziah saw that her son was dead, she arose and destroyed all the seed royal. But Jehosheba, the daughter of king Joram, sister of Ahaziah, took Joash the son of Ahaziah, and stole him away from among the king's sons that were slain, even him and his nurse, and put them in the bed-chamber; and they hid him from Athaliah, so that he was not slain. And he was with her hid in the house of Yehovah six years; and Athaliah reigned over the land. And n the seventh year Jehoiada sent and fetched the captains over hundreds, of the Carites and of the guard, and brought them to him into the house of Yehovah; and he made a covenant with them, and took an oath of them in the house of Yehovah, and showed them the king's son.
יְהוֹאָשׁ Y'ho'ash (Jehoash)		40	879	2 Kings 12:1-2 Jehoash was seven years old when he began to reign. In the seventh year of Jehu began Jehoash to reign; and he reigned forty years in Yerushalam; and his mother's name was Zibiah of Beer-sheba.

Continued on next page

Judah	Israel	Years	BCE	Reference
	יְהוֹאָחָז Y'ho'ah'khaz (Jehoahaz)	17	816	2 Kings 13:1 In the three and twentieth year of Joash the son of Ahaziah, king of Judah, Jehoahaz the son of Jehu began to reign over Israel in Samaria, and reigned seventeen years.
	יְהוֹאָשׁ Y'ho'ash (Jehoash)	16	799	2 Kings 13:10 In the thirty and seventh year of Joash king of Judah began Jehoash the son of Jehoahaz to reign over Israel in Samaria, and reigned sixteen years.
אֲמַצְיָהוּ Uh'muhtz'yah'hu (Amaziah)		29	839	2 Kings 14:1-2 In the second year of Joash son of Joahaz king of Israel began Amaziah the son of Joash king of Judah to reign. He was twenty and five years old when he began to reign; and he reigned twenty and nine years in Yerushalam; and his mother's name was Jehoaddan of Yerushalam.
	יָרָבְעָם Yah'rahv'ahm (Jeroboam)	41	783	2 Kings 14:23 In the fifteenth year of Amaziah the son of Joash king of Judah Jeroboam the son of Joash king of Israel began to reign in Samaria, and reigned forty and one years.

Continued on next page

Judah	Israel	Years	BCE	Reference
עֲזַרְיָה Uh'zar'yah (Azariah) עֻזִּיָּהוּ Uu'zee'yah'hu (Uzziah)		52	810	2 Kings 15:1-2 In the twenty and seventh year of Jeroboam king of Israel began Azariah son of Amaziah king of Judah to reign. Sixteen years old was he when he began to reign; and he reigned two and fifty years in Yerushalam; and his mother's name was Jecoliah of Yerushalam. 2 Chronicles 26:1-5 And all the people of Judah took Uzziah, who was sixteen years old, and made him king in the room of his father Amaziah. He built Eloth, and restored it to Judah, after that the king slept with his fathers. Sixteen years old was Uzziah when he began to reign; and he reigned fifty and two years in Yerushalam; and his mother's name was Jecoliah of Yerushalam. And he did that, which was right in the eyes of Yehovah, according to all that his father Amaziah had done. And he set himself to seek God in the days of Zechariah, who had understanding in the vision of God; and as long as he sought Yehovah, God made him to prosper. 2 Chronicles 26:22-23 Now the rest of the acts of Uzziah, first and last, did Isaiah the prophet, the son of Amoz, write. So Uzziah slept with his fathers; and they buried him with his fathers in the field of burial which belonged to the kings; for they said: 'He is a leper'; and Jotham his son reigned in his stead.

Continued on next page

Judah	Israel	Years	BCE	Reference
	זְכַרְיָהוּ Z'char'yah'hu (Zechariah)	6 Months	742	2 Kings 15:8 In the thirty and eighth year of Azariah king of Judah did Zechariah the son of Jeroboam reign over Israel in Samaria six months.
	שַׁלּוּם Sha'luum (Shallum)	1 Month	742	2 Kings 15:13 Shallum the son of Jabesh began to reign in the nine and thirtieth year of Uzziah king of Judah; and he reigned the space of a month in Samaria.
	מְנַחֵם M'nuh'khaim (Menahem)	10	742	2 Kings 15:17 In the nine and thirtieth year of Azariah king of Judah began Menahem the son of Gadi to reign over Israel, and reigned ten years in Samaria.
	פְּקַחְיָה P'kukh'yah (Pekahiah)	2	732	2 Kings 15:23 In the fiftieth year of Azariah king of Judah Pekahiah the son of Menahem began to reign over Israel in Samaria, and reigned two years.
יוֹתָם Yo'thahm (Jotham)		16	758	2 Kings 15:32-33 In the second year of Pekah the son of Remaliah king of Israel began Jotham the son of Uzziah king of Judah to reign. Five and twenty years old was he when he began to reign; and he reigned sixteen years in Yerushalam; and his mother's name was Jerusha the daughter of Zadok.

Continued on next page

Judah	Israel	Years	BCE	Reference
אָחָז Ah'khaz (Ahaz)		16	742	2 Kings 16:1-2 In the seventeenth year of Pekah the son of Remaliah Ahaz the son of Jotham king of Judah began to reign. Twenty years old was Ahaz when he began to reign; and he reigned sixteen years in Yerushalam; and he did not that which was right in the eyes of Yehovah his God, like David his father.
	הוֹשֵׁעַ Ho'shay'uh (Hoshea)	9	730	2 Kings 17:1, 6a In the twelfth year of Ahaz king of Judah began Hoshea the son of Elah to reign in Samaria over Israel, and reigned nine years. **In the ninth year of Hoshea, the king of Assyria took Samaria, and carried Israel away unto Assyria,...**
חִזְקִיָּה Kheez'kee'yah (Hezekiah)		29	726	2 Kings 18:1-2 Now it came to pass in the third year of Hoshea son of Elah king of Israel, that Hezekiah the son of Ahaz king of Judah began to reign. Twenty and five years old was he when he began to reign; and he reigned twenty and nine years in Yerushalam; and his mother's name was Abi the daughter of Zechariah.
מְנַשֶּׁה M'nuh'sheh (Manasseh)		55	697	2 Kings 21:1 Manasseh was twelve years old when he began to reign; and he reigned five and fifty years in Yerushalam; and his mother's name was Hephzi-bah.

Continued on next page

Judah	Israel	Years	BCE	Reference
אָמוֹן Ah'moan (Amon)		2	642	2 Kings 21:19 Amon was twenty and two years old when he began to reign; and he reigned two years in Yerushalam; and his mother's name was Meshullemeth the daughter of Haruz of Jotbah.
יֹאשִׁיָּהוּ Yo'shee'yah'hu (Josiah)		31	640	2 Kings 22:1 Josiah was eight years old when he began to reign; and he reigned thirty and one years in Yerushalam; and his mother's name was Jedidah the daughter of Adaiah of Bozkath.
יְהוֹאָחָז Y'ho'ah'khaz (Jehoahaz)		3 Months	609	2 Kings 23:31 Jehoahaz was twenty and three years old when he began to reign; and he reigned three months in Yerushalam; and his mother's name was Hamutal the daughter of Jeremiah of Libnah.
אֶלְיָקִים El'yah'keem (Eliakim) ——————— יְהוֹיָקִים Y'ho'yah'keem (Jehoiakim)		11	608	2 Kings 23:34, 36 And Pharaoh-necoh made Eliakim the son of Josiah king in the room of Josiah his father, and changed his name to Jehoiakim; but he took Jehoahaz away; and he came to Egypt, and died there. Jehoiakim was twenty and five years old when he began to reign; and he reigned eleven years in Yerushalam; and his mother's name was Zebudah the daughter of Pedaiah of Rumah.

Continued on next page

Judah	Israel	Years	BCE	Reference
יְהוֹיָכִין Y'ho'yah'cheen (Jehoiachin)		3 Months	597	2 Kings 24:8 Jehoiachin was eighteen years old when he began to reign; and he reigned in Yerushalam three months; and his mother's name was Nehushta the daughter of Elnathan of Yerushalam.
מַתַּנְיָה Muh'thun'yah (Mattaniah) ——————— צִדְקִיָּהוּ Tzeed'kee'yah'hu (Zedekiah)		11	597	2 Kings 24:17-18 And the king of Babylon made Mattaniah his father's brother king in his stead, and changed his name to Zedekiah. Zedekiah was twenty and one years old when he began to reign; and he reigned eleven years in Yerushalam; and his mother's name was Hamutal the daughter of Jeremiah of Libnah.

Continued on next page

Judah	Israel	Years	BCE	Reference
			586	2 Kings 25:1-2, 8-9 And it came to pass in the ninth year of his reign, in the tenth month, in the tenth day of the month, that Nebuchadnezzar king of Babylon came, he and all his army, against Yerushalam, and encamped against it; and they built forts against it round about. So the city was besieged unto the eleventh year of king Zedekiah. Now in the fifth month, on the seventh day of the month, which was the nineteenth year of king Nebuchadnezzar, king of Babylon, came Nebuzaradan the captain of the guard, a servant of the king of Babylon, unto Yerushalam. **And he burnt the house of Yehovah, and the king's house; and all the houses of Yerushalam, even every great man's house, burnt he with fire.**

Prophets (By Their Books)

Prophet	Reference
מֹשֶׁה Mo'sheh (Moses) ——————— אַהֲרֹן Uh'huh'roan (Aaron)	Exodus 7:1-2 And Yehovah said unto Moses: 'See, I have set thee in God's stead to Pharaoh; and Aaron thy brother shall be thy prophet. Thou shalt speak all that I command thee; and Aaron thy brother shall speak unto Pharaoh, that he let the children of Israel go out of his land.
יְהוֹשֻׁעַ Y'ho'shoo'uh (Joshua)	Joshua 1:1-8 Now it came to pass after the death of Moses the servant of Yehovah, that Yehovah spoke unto Joshua the son of Nun, Moses' minister, saying: 'Moses My servant is dead; now therefore arise, go over this Jordan, thou, and all this people, unto the land which I do give to them, even to the children of Israel. Every place that the sole of your foot shall tread upon, to you have I given it, as I spoke unto Moses. From the wilderness, and this Lebanon, even unto the great river, the river Euphrates, all the land of the Hittites, and unto the Great Sea toward the going down of the sun, shall be your border. There shall not any man be able to stand before thee all the days of thy life; as I was with Moses, so I will be with thee; I will not fail thee, nor forsake thee. Be strong and of good courage; for thou shalt cause this people to inherit the land which I swore unto their fathers to give them. Only be strong and very courageous, to observe to do according to all the Torah, which Moses My servant commanded thee; turn not from it to the right hand or to the left, that thou mayest have good success whithersoever thou goest. This book of the Torah shall not depart out of thy mouth, but thou shalt meditate therein day and night, that thou mayest observe to do according to all that is written therein; for then thou shalt make thy ways prosperous, and then thou shalt have good success.

Continued on next page

Prophet	Reference
יְשַׁעְיָהוּ Y'shuh'yah'hu (Isaiah)	Isaiah 1:1 The vision of Isaiah the son of Amoz, which he saw concerning Judah and Yerushalam, in the days of Uzziah, Jotham, Ahaz, and Hezekiah, kings of Judah.
יִרְמְיָהוּ Yeer'm'yah'hu (Jeremiah)	Jeremiah 1:1-3 The words of Jeremiah the son of Hilkiah, of the priests that were in Anathoth in the land of Benjamin, to whom the word of Yehovah came in the days of Josiah the son of Amon, king of Judah, in the thirteenth year of his reign. It came also in the days of Jehoiakim the son of Josiah, king of Judah, unto the end of the eleventh year of Zedekiah the son of Josiah, king of Judah, unto the carrying away of Yerushalam captive in the fifth month.
יְחֶזְקֵאל Y'khez'kayl (Ezekiel)	Ezekiel 1:1-3 Now it came to pass in the thirtieth year, in the fourth month, in the fifth day of the month, as I was among the captives by the river Chebar that the heavens were opened, and I saw visions of God. In the fifth day of the month, which was the fifth year of king Jehoiachin's captivity, the word of Yehovah came expressly unto Ezekiel the priest, the son of Buzi, in the land of the Chaldeans by the river Chebar; and the hand of Yehovah was there upon him.
הוֹשֵׁעַ Ho'shay'uh (Hosea)	Hosea 1:1 The word of Yehovah that came unto Hosea the son of Beeri, in the days of Uzziah, Jotham, Ahaz, and Hezekiah, kings of Judah, and in the days of Jeroboam the son of Joash, king of Israel.
יוֹאֵל Yo'ale (Joel)	Joel 1:1 The word of Yehovah that came to Joel the son of Pethuel.

Continued on next page

Prophet	Reference
עָמוֹס Ah'mose (Amos)	Amos 1:1 The words of Amos, who was among the herdmen of Tekoa, which he saw concerning Israel in the days of Uzziah king of Judah, and in the days of Jeroboam the son of Joash king of Israel, two years before the earthquake.
עֹבַדְיָה Oh'vud'yah (Obadiah)	Obadiah 1:1 The vision of Obadiah. Thus saith the Lord GOD [Adonai Yehovi] concerning Edom: We have heard a message from Yehovah, and an ambassador is sent among the nations: 'Arise ye, and let us rise up against her in battle.'
יוֹנָה Yo'nah (Jonah)	2 Kings 14:23-25 In the fifteenth year of Amaziah the son of Joash king of Judah Jeroboam the son of Joash king of Israel began to reign in Samaria, and reigned forty and one years. And he did that which was evil in the sight of Yehovah; he departed not from all the sins of Jeroboam the son of Nebat, wherewith he made Israel to sin. He restored the border of Israel from the entrance of Hamath unto the sea of the Arabah, according to the word of Yehovah, the God of Israel, which He spoke by the hand of His servant Jonah the son of Amittai, the prophet, who was of Gath-hepher. Jonah 1:1-2 Now the word of Yehovah came unto Jonah the son of Amittai, saying: 'Arise, go to Nineveh, that great city, and proclaim against it; for their wickedness is come up before Me.'
מִיכָה Mee'chah (Micah)	Micah 1:1 The word of Yehovah that came to Micah the Morashtite in the days of Jotham, Ahaz, and Hezekiah, kings of Judah, which he saw concerning Samaria and Yerushalam.

Continued on next page

Prophet	Reference
נַחוּם Nuh'khoom (Nahum)	Nahum 1:1 The burden of Nineveh. The book of the vision of Nahum the Elkoshite.
חֲבַקּוּק Khuh'vuh'kook (Habakkuk)	Habakkuk 1:1 The burden which Habakkuk the prophet did see.
צְפַנְיָה Tz'phun'yah (Zephaniah)	Zephaniah 1:1 The word of Yehovah which came unto Zephaniah the son of Cushi, the son of Gedaliah, the son of Amariah, the son of Hezekiah, in the days of Josiah the son of Amon, king of Judah.
חַגַּי Khuh'gai (Haggai)	Haggai 1:1 In the second year of Darius the king, in the sixth month, in the first day of the month, came the word of Yehovah by Haggai the prophet unto Zerubbabel the son of Shealtiel, governor of Judah, and to Joshua the son of Jehozadak, the high priest, saying:
זְכַרְיָה Z'char'yah (Zechariah)	Zechariah 1:1 In the eighth month, in the second year of Darius, came the word of Yehovah unto Zechariah the son of Berechiah, the son of Iddo, the prophet, saying:
מַלְאָכִי Muhl'ah'chee (Malachi)	Malachi 1:1 The burden of the word of Yehovah to Israel by Malachi.

Continued on next page

Prophet	Reference
דָּנִיֵּאל Dah'nee'yale (Daniel)	Daniel 1:1-6 In the third year of the reign of Jehoiakim king of Judah came Nebuchacnezzar king of Babylon unto Yerushalam, and besieged it. And the Lord gave Jehoiakim king of Judah into his hand, with part of the vessels of the house of God; and he carried them into the land of Shinar to the house of his god, and the vessels he brought into the treasure-house of his god. And the king spoke unto Ashpenaz his chief officer, that he should bring in certain of the children of Israel, and of the seed royal, and of the nobles, youths in whom was no blemish, but fair to look on, and skilful in all wisdom, and skilful in knowledge, and discerning in thought, and such as had ability to stand in the king's palace; and that he should teach them the learning and the tongue of the Chaldeans. And the king appointed for them a daily portion of the king's food, and of the wine which he drank, and that they should be nourished three years; that at the end thereof they might stand before the king. Now among these were, of the children of Judah, Daniel, Hananiah, Mishael, and Azariah. --- Note: According to Judaism, Daniel was not a prophet, mainly because his visions were not intended to be proclaimed to people but written for the future.[4]

[4]Tracey R. Rich, 'Prophets and Prophecy,' Judaism 101, accessed 29 Oct 2025, https://www.jewfaq.org/prophets.

Other Prophets

Prophet	Reference
אַבְרָהָם Uv'rah'hahm (Abraham)	Genesis 17:4-7 'As for Me, behold, My covenant is with thee, and thou shalt be the father of a multitude of nations. Neither shall thy name any more be called Abram, but thy name shall be Abraham; for the father of a multitude of nations have I made thee. And I will make thee exceeding fruitful, and I will make nations of thee, and kings shall come out of thee. And I will establish My covenant between Me and thee and thy seed after thee throughout their generations for an everlasting covenant, to be a God unto thee and to thy seed after thee. Genesis 20:6-7 And God said unto him in the dream: 'Yea, I know that in the simplicity of thy heart thou hast done this, and I also withheld thee from sinning against Me. Therefore suffered I thee not to touch her. Now therefore restore the man's wife; for he is a prophet, and he shall pray for thee, and thou shalt live; and if thou restore her not, know thou that thou shalt surely die, thou, and all that are thine.'
מִרְיָם Meer'yam Miriam	Exodus 15:20-21 And Miriam the prophetess, the sister of Aaron, took a timbrel in her hand; and all the women went out after her with timbrels and with dances. And Miriam sang unto them: Sing ye to Yehovah, for He is highly exalted: the horse and his rider hath He thrown into the sea.

Continued on next page

Prophet	Reference
פִּינְחָס Peen'khahs (Phineas)	Numbers 25:6-13 And, behold, one of the children of Israel came and brought unto his brethren a Midianitish woman in the sight of Moses, and in the sight of all the congregation of the children of Israel, while they were weeping at the door of the tent of meeting. And when Phinehas, the son of Eleazar, the son of Aaron the priest, saw it, he rose up from the midst of the congregation, and took a spear in his hand. And he went after the man of Israel into the chamber, and thrust both of them through, the man of Israel, and the woman through her belly. So the plague was stayed from the children of Israel. And those that died by the plague were twenty and four thousand. And Yehovah spoke unto Moses, saying: 'Phinehas, the son of Eleazar, the son of Aaron the priest, hath turned My wrath away from the children of Israel, in that he was very jealous for My sake among them, so that I consumed not the children of Israel in My jealousy. Wherefore say: Behold, I give unto him My covenant of peace; and it shall be unto him, and to his seed after him, the covenant of an everlasting priesthood; because he was jealous for his God, and made atonement for the children of Israel.'
דְּבוֹרָה D'voh'rah (Deborah)	Judges 4:4-6 Now Deborah, a prophetess, the wife of Lappidoth, she judged Israel at that time. And she sat under the palm-tree of Deborah between Ramah and Beth-el in the hill-country of Ephraim; and the children of Israel came up to her for judgment. And she sent and called Barak the son of Abinoam out of Kedesh-naphtali, and said unto him: 'Hath not Yehovah, the God of Israel, commanded, saying: Go and draw toward mount Tabor, and take with thee ten thousand men of the children of Naphtali and of the children of Zebulun?

Continued on next page

Prophet	Reference
עֵלִי Ei'lee (Eli)	1 Samuel 1:15-17, 20 And Hannah answered and said: 'No, my lord, I am a woman of a sorrowful spirit; I have drunk neither wine nor strong drink, but I poured out my soul before Yehovah. Count not thy handmaid for a wicked woman: for out of the abundance of my complaint and my vexation have I spoken hitherto.' Then Eli answered and said: 'Go in peace, and the God of Israel grant thy petition that thou hast asked of Him.' And it came to pass, when the time was come about, that Hannah conceived, and bore a son; and she called his name Samuel: 'because I have asked him of Yehovah.'
גָּד Gahd (Gad)	1 Samuel 22:5 And the prophet Gad said unto David: 'Abide not in the stronghold; depart, and get thee into the land of Judah.' Then David departed, and came into the forest of Hereth. 2 Samuel 22:11-12 And when David rose up in the morning, the word of Yehovah came unto the prophet Gad, David's seer, saying: 'Go and speak unto David: Thus saith Yehovah: I lay upon thee three things; choose thee one of them, that I may do it unto thee.'

Continued on next page

Prophet	Reference
נָתָן Nah'thahn (Nathan)	2 Samuel 7:1-7 And it came to pass, when the king dwelt in his house, and Yehovah had given him rest from all his enemies round about, that the king said unto Nathan the prophet: 'See now, I dwell in a house of cedar, but the ark of God dwelleth within curtains.' And Nathan said to the king: 'Go, do all that is in thy heart; for Yehovah is with thee.' And it came to pass the same night, that the word of Yehovah came unto Nathan, saying: Go and tell My servant David: Thus saith Yehovah: Shalt thou build Me a house for Me to dwell in? or I have not dwelt in a house since the day that I brought up the children of Israel out of Egypt, even to this day, but have walked in a tent and in a tabernacle. In all places wherein I have walked among all the children of Israel, spoke I a word with any of the tribes of Israel, whom I commanded to feed My people Israel, saying: Why have ye not built Me a house of cedar?
נָתָן Nah'thahn (Nathan) ——— אֲחִיָּה Uh'khee'yah (Ahijah) ——— יֶעְדּוֹ Yeh'doh (Jedo / Iddo)	2 Chronicles 9:29 Now the rest of the acts of Solomon, first and last, are they not written in the words of Nathan the prophet, and in the prophecy of Ahijah the Shilonite, and in the visions of Jedo the seer concerning Jeroboam the son of Nebat?

Continued on next page

Prophet	Reference
שְׁמַעְיָה Shmuh'yah Shemaiah ――――― עִדּוֹ Ee'doh (Iddo)	**1 Kings 12:22-24** But the word of God came unto Shemaiah the man of God, saying: 'Speak unto Rehoboam the son of Solomon, king of Judah, and unto all the house of Judah and Benjamin, and to the rest of the people, saying: Thus saith Yehovah: Ye shall not go up, nor fight against your brethren the children of Israel; return every man to his house; for this thing is of Me.' So they hearkened unto the word of Yehovah, and returned and went their way, according to the word of Yehovah. **2 Chronicles 12:15** Now the acts of Rehoboam, first and last, are they not written in the histories of Shemaiah the prophet and of Iddo the seer, after the manner of genealogies? And there were wars between Rehoboam and Jeroboam continually. **2 Chronicles 13:22** And the rest of the acts of Abijah, and his ways, and his sayings, are written in the commentary of the prophet Iddo.
מִיכָיְהוּ Mee'chahy'hu (Micaiah)	**1 Kings 22:8** And the king of Israel said unto Jehoshaphat: 'There is yet one man by whom we may inquire of Yehovah, Micaiah the son of Imlah; but I hate him; for he doth not prophesy good concerning me, but evil.' And Jehoshaphat said: 'Let not the king say so.' **2 Chronicles 18:7** And the king of Israel said unto Jehoshaphat: 'There is yet one man by whom we may inquire of Yehovah; but I hate him; for he never prophesieth good concerning me, but always evil; the same is Micaiah the son of Imla.' And Jehoshaphat said: 'Let not the king say so.'

Continued on next page

Prophet	Reference
אֲחִיָּה Uh'khee'yah (Ahijah)	1 Kings 11:29-36 And it came to pass at that time, when Jeroboam went out of Yerushalam, that the prophet Ahijah the Shilonite found him in the way; now Ahijah had clad himself with a new garment; and they two were alone in the field. And Ahijah laid hold of the new garment that was on him, and rent it in twelve pieces. And he said to Jeroboam: 'Take thee ten pieces; for thus saith Yehovah, the God of Israel: Behold, I will rend the kingdom out of the hand of Solomon, and will give ten tribes to thee-- but he shall have one tribe, for My servant David's sake, and for Yerushalam's sake, the city which I have chosen out of all the tribes of Israel-- because that they have forsaken Me, and have worshipped Ashtoreth the goddess of the Zidonians, Chemosh the god of Moab, and Milcom the god of the children of Ammon; and they have not walked in My ways, to do that which is right in Mine eyes, and to keep My statutes and Mine ordinances, as did David his father. Howbeit I will not take the whole kingdom out of his hand; but I will make him prince all the days of his life, for David My servant's sake, whom I chose, because he kept My commandments and My statutes; but I will take the kingdom out of his son's hand, and will give it unto thee, even ten tribes. And unto his son will I give one tribe, that David My servant may have a lamp alway before Me in Yerushalam, the city which I have chosen Me to put My name there.

Continued on next page

Prophet	Reference
יֵהוּא Yay'hu (Jehu)	1 Kings 16:1-4 And the word of Yehovah came to Jehu the son of Hanani against Baasa, saying: 'Forasmuch as I exalted thee out of the dust, and made thee prince over My people Israel; and thou hast walked in the way of Jeroboam, and hast made My people Israel to sin, to provoke Me with their sins; behold, I will utterly sweep away Baasa and his house; and I will make thy house like the house of Jeroboam the son of Nebat. Him that dieth of Baasa in the city shall the dogs eat; and him that dieth of his in the field shall the fowls of the air eat.' 2 Chronicles 19:2-3 And Jehu the son of Hanani the seer went out to meet him, and said to king Jehoshaphat: 'Shouldest thou help the wicked, and love them that hate Yehovah? for this thing wrath is upon thee from before Yehovah. Nevertheless there are good things found in thee, in that thou hast put away the Asheroth out of the land, and hast set thy heart to seek God.'
עֲזַרְיָהוּ Uh'zar'yah'hu (Azariah)	2 Chronicles 15:1-4 And the spirit of God came upon Azariah the son of Oded; and he went out to meet Asa, and said unto him: 'Hear ye me, Asa, and all Judah and Benjamin: Yehovah is with you, while ye are with Him; and if ye seek Him, He will be found of you; but if ye forsake Him, He will forsake you. Now for long seasons Israel was without the true God, and without a teaching priest, and without Torah; but when in their distress they turned unto Yehovah, the God of Israel, and sought Him, He was found of them. 2 Chronicles 15:8 And when Asa heard these words, even the prophecy of Oded the prophet, he took courage, and put away the detestable things out of all the land of Judah and Benjamin, and out of the cities which he had taken from the hill-country of Ephraim; and he renewed the altar of Yehovah, that was before the porch of Yehovah.

Continued on next page

Prophet	Reference
יַחֲזִיאֵל Yuh'khuh'zee'ail (Jahaziel)	2 Chronicles 20:14-18 Then upon Jahaziel the son of Zechariah, the son of Benaiah, the son of Jeiel, the son of Mattaniah, the Levite, of the sons of Asaph, came the spirit of Yehovah in the midst of the congregation; and he said: 'Hearken ye, all Judah, and ye inhabitants of Yerushalam, and thou king Jehoshaphat: thus saith Yehovah unto you: Fear not ye, neither be dismayed by reason of this great multitude; for the battle is not yours, but God's. To-morrow go ye down against them; behold, they come up by the ascent of Ziz; and ye shall find them at the end of the valley, before the wilderness of Jeruel. Ye shall not need to fight in this battle; set yourselves, stand ye still, and see the salvation of Yehovah with you, O Judah and Yerushalam; fear not, nor be dismayed; to-morrow go out against them; for Yehovah is with you.' And Jehoshaphat bowed his head with his face to the ground; and all Judah and the inhabitants of Yerushalam fell down before Yehovah, worshipping Yehovah.
אֱלִיעֶזֶר Eh'lee'eh'zer (Eliezer)	2 Chronicles 20:37 Then Eliezer the son of Dodavahu of Mareshah prophesied against Jehoshaphat, saying: 'Because thou hast joined thyself with Ahaziah, Yehovah hath made a breach in thy works.' And the ships were broken, that they were not able to go to Tarshish.

Continued on next page

Prophet	Reference
אֵלִיָּ֫הוּ Ei'lee'yah'hu (Elijah)	**1 Kings 17:1** And Elijah the Tishbite, who was of the settlers of Gilead, said unto Ahab: 'As Yehovah, the God of Israel, liveth, before whom I stand, there shall not be dew nor rain these years, but according to my word.' **1 Kings 18:1** And it came to pass after many days, that the word of Yehovah came to Elijah, in the third year, saying: 'Go, show thyself unto Ahab, and I will send rain upon the land.' **1 Kings 19:13-16** And it was so, when Elijah heard it, that he wrapped his face in his mantle, and went out, and stood in the entrance of the cave. And, behold, there came a voice unto him, and said: 'What doest thou here, Elijah?' And he said: 'I have been very jealous for Yehovah, the God of hosts; for the children of Israel have forsaken Thy covenant, thrown down Thine altars, and slain Thy prophets with the sword; and I, even I only, am left; and they seek my life, to take it away.' And Yehovah said unto him: 'Go, return on thy way to the wilderness of Damascus; and when thou comest, thou shalt anoint Hazael to be king over Aram; and Jehu the son of Nimshi shalt thou anoint to be king over Israel; and Elisha the son of Shaphat of Abel-meholah shalt thou anoint to be prophet in thy room. And it shall come to pass, that him that escapeth from the sword of Hazael shall Jehu slay; and him that escapeth from the sword of Jehu shall Elisha slay.

Continued on next page

Prophet	Reference
אֱלִישָׁע Eh'lee'shah (Elisha)	1 Kings 19:19 So he departed thence, and found Elisha the son of Shaphat, who was plowing, with twelve yoke of oxen before him, and he with the twelfth; and Elijah passed over unto him, and cast his mantle upon him. 2 Kings 2:11-14 And it came to pass, as they still went on, and talked, that, behold, there appeared a chariot of fire, and horses of fire, which parted them both asunder; and Elijah went up by a whirlwind into heaven. And Elisha saw it, and he cried: 'My father, my father, the chariots of Israel and the horsemen thereof!' And he saw him no more; and he took hold of his own clothes, and rent them in two pieces. He took up also the mantle of Elijah that fell from him, and went back, and stood by the bank of the Jordan. And he took the mantle of Elijah that fell from him, and smote the waters, and said: 'Where is Yehovah, the God of Elijah?' and when he also had smitten the waters, they were divided hither and thither; and Elisha went over.

Continued on next page

Prophet	Reference
חֻלְדָּה Khul'dah (Huldah)	2 Kings 22:14-20 So Hilkiah the priest, and Ahikam, and Achbor, and Shaphan, and Asaiah, went unto Huldah the prophetess, the wife of Shallum the son of Tikvah, the son of Harhas, keeper of the wardrobe--now she dwelt in Yerushalam in the second quarter-- and they spoke with her. And she said unto them: 'Thus saith Yehovah, the God of Israel: Tell ye the man that sent you unto me: Thus saith Yehovah: Behold, I will bring evil upon this place, and upon the inhabitants thereof, even all the words of the book which the king of Judah hath read; because they have forsaken Me, and have offered unto other gods, that they might provoke Me with all the work of their hands; therefore My wrath shall be kindled against this place, and it shall not be quenched. But unto the king of Judah, who sent you to inquire of Yehovah, thus shall ye say to him: Thus saith Yehovah, the God of Israel: As touching the words which thou hast heard, because thy heart was tender, and thou didst humble thyself before Yehovah, when thou heardest what I spoke against this place, and against the inhabitants thereof, that they should become an astonishment and a curse, and hast rent thy clothes, and wept before Me, I also have heard thee, saith Yehovah. Therefore, behold, I will gather thee to thy fathers, and thou shalt be gathered to thy grave in peace, neither shall thine eyes see all the evil which I will bring upon this place.' And they brought back word unto the king.

Continued on next page

Prophet	Reference
אוּרִיָּהוּ Uu'ree'yah'hu (Uriah)	Jeremiah 26:20-23 And there was also a man that prophesied in the name of Yehovah, Uriah the son of Shemaiah of Kiriath-jearim; and he prophesied against this city and against this land according to all the words of Jeremiah; and when Jehoiakim the king, with all his mighty men, and all the princes, heard his words, the king sought to put him to death; but when Uriah heard it, he was afraid, and fled, and went into Egypt; and Jehoiakim the king sent men into Egypt, Elnathan the son of Achbor, and certain men with him, into Egypt; and they fetched forth Uriah out of Egypt, and brought him unto Jehoiakim the king; who slew him with the sword, and cast his dead body into the graves of the children of the people.

I have provided the tables, above, giving the year BCE of the **Kings,** years of rest for **Judges** and a list of **Prophets** (first with books named after them and followed by 'Other Prophets'). There is at least one Judge, like Deborah, acknowledged as a prophetess, who I have repeated under 'Other Prophets.'

It is my hope that showing these tables gives a perspective of times with Scriptural references which will help bring a better understanding of leadership in ancient Israel in addition to the list of the High Priests shown in an earlier chapter.

Seek Yehovah

55 <u>6</u> **Seek ye Yehovah while He may be found, call ye upon Him while He is near;**

<u>7</u> **Let the wicked forsake his way, and the man of iniquity his thoughts; and let him return unto Yehovah, and He will have compassion upon him, and to our God, for He will abundantly pardon.**

[Isaiah 55:6-7 The Pill Tanakh]

נה ו דִּרְשׁוּ יְהֹוָה בְּהִמָּצְאוֹ קְרָאֻהוּ בִּהְיוֹתוֹ
קָרוֹב:

55 6 Seek ye Yehovah while He may be found, call ye upon Him while He is near;

ז יַעֲזֹב רָשָׁע דַּרְכּוֹ וְאִישׁ אָוֶן מַחְשְׁבֹתָיו וְיָשֹׁב
אֶל־יְהֹוָה וִירַחֲמֵהוּ וְאֶל־אֱלֹהֵינוּ כִּי־יַרְבֶּה
לִסְלוֹחַ:

7 Let the wicked forsake his way, and the man of iniquity his thoughts; and let him return unto Yehovah, and He will have compassion upon him, and to our God, for He will abundantly pardon.

ח כִּי לֹא מַחְשְׁבוֹתַי מַחְשְׁבוֹתֵיכֶם וְלֹא דַרְכֵיכֶם
דְּרָכָי נְאֻם יְהֹוָה:

8 For My thoughts are not your thoughts, neither are your ways My ways, saith Yehovah.

ט כִּי־גָבְהוּ שָׁמַיִם מֵאָרֶץ כֵּן גָּבְהוּ דְרָכַי

מִדַּרְכֵיכֶם וּמַחְשְׁבֹתַי מִמַּחְשְׁבֹתֵיכֶם:

9 For as the heavens are higher than the earth, so are My ways higher than your ways, and My thoughts than your thoughts.
[Isaiah 55:6-9 The Pill Tanakh]

Repentance!

In Isaiah 55:7, *repenting* means וְיָשֹׁב אֶל־יְהֹוָה **and let him return to Yehovah.**

But what is **'returning to Yehovah?'**

ה ג   בְּטַח אֶל־יְהֹוָה בְּכָל־לִבֶּךָ וְאֶל־בִּינָתְךָ
אַל־תִּשָּׁעֵן:

3 5 Trust in Yehovah with all thy heart, and lean not upon thine own understanding.

ו בְּכָל־דְּרָכֶיךָ דָעֵהוּ וְהוּא יְיַשֵּׁר אֹרְחֹתֶיךָ:

6 In all thy ways acknowledge Him, and He will direct thy paths.

ז אַל־תְּהִי חָכָם בְּעֵינֶיךָ יְרָא אֶת־יְהֹוָה וְסוּר
מֵרָע:

7 Be not wise in thine own eyes; fear Yehovah, and depart from evil;

יג אַשְׁרֵי אָדָם מָצָא חָכְמָה וְאָדָם יָפִיק תְּבוּנָה:

13 Happy is the man that findeth wisdom, and the man that obtaineth understanding.

יד כִּי טוֹב סַחְרָהּ מִסְּחַר־כָּסֶף וּמֵחָרוּץ
תְּבוּאָתָהּ:

<u>14</u> For the merchandise of it is better than the merchandise of silver, and the gain thereof than fine gold.

יֵהּ יְקָרָה הִיא מִפְּנִינִים וְכָל־חֲפָצֶיךָ לֹא יִשְׁווּ־בָהּ:

<u>15</u> She is more precious than rubies; and all the things thou canst desire are not to be compared unto her.

יֵז אֹרֶךְ יָמִים בִּימִינָהּ בִּשְׂמֹאולָהּ עֹשֶׁר וְכָבוֹד:

<u>16</u> Length of days is in her right hand; in her left hand are riches and honour.

יֵז דְּרָכֶיהָ דַרְכֵי־נֹעַם וְכָל־נְתִיבוֹתֶיהָ שָׁלוֹם:

<u>17</u> Her ways are ways of pleasantness, and all her paths are peace.

יֵח עֵץ־חַיִּים הִיא לַמַּחֲזִיקִים בָּהּ וְתֹמְכֶיהָ מְאֻשָּׁר:

<u>18</u> She is a tree of life to them that lay hold upon her, and happy is every one that holdest her fast.
[Proverbs 3:5-7, 13-18 The Pill Tanakh]

You can see that I have used passages from Scripture to reinforce points I have wanted to express. Proverbs 3:5 certainly sets the requirement of repentance succinctly!

3 <u>5</u> Trust in Yehovah with all thy heart, and lean not upon thine own understanding. [Proverbs 3:5 The Pill Tanakh]

Can anyone come into a personal relationship with יְהוָה Yehovah _without repenting first, with humility_?

וֹ ח הִגִּיד לְךָ אָדָם מַה־טּוֹב וּמָה־יְהוָה דּוֹרֵשׁ
מִמְּךָ כִּי אִם־עֲשׂוֹת מִשְׁפָּט וְאַהֲבַת חֶסֶד וְהַצְנֵעַ
לֶכֶת עִם־אֱלֹהֶיךָ:

6 8 It hath been told thee, O man, what is
good, and what Yehovah doth require of thee:
only to do justly, and to love mercy, and to walk
humbly with thy God. [Micah 6:8 The Pill Tanakh]

ב ג בַּקְּשׁוּ אֶת־יְהוָה כָּל־עַנְוֵי הָאָרֶץ אֲשֶׁר מִשְׁפָּטוֹ
פָּעָלוּ בַּקְּשׁוּ־צֶדֶק בַּקְּשׁוּ עֲנָוָה אוּלַי תִּסָּתְרוּ בְּיוֹם
אַף־יְהוָה:

2 3 Seek ye Yehovah, all ye humble of the
earth, that have executed His ordinance;
seek righteousness, seek humility. It may be
ye shall be hid in the day of Yehovah's anger.
[Zephaniah 2:3 The Pill Tanakh]

Obviously, anyone who was raised in a family with even a
modicum of religious upbringing will have a knowledge of "God."
The three major world religions of Judaism, Christianity and Islam
will have contributed to that understanding. Certainly, that does
not mean that those persons have a meaningful relationship with
the Almighty, but perhaps nothing more than a general knowledge.

Of course, each of those religious systems provide methodologies
for greater faith, such as a devotion to study or even having a
discipline of saying certain prayers, wearing religious attire, etc.

No doubt there are some people who have an understanding of
God after experiencing some sort of encounter that changes their
life. That experience may be "supernatural" like the people of
Israel in Elijah's day, who, **after seeing the sacrifice on an altar
soaked with water saw it totally consumed by the fire of
Yehovah** (1 Kings 18)! They said, **'Yehovah, He is God;
Yehovah, He is God.'**

יח לח וַתִּפֹּל אֵשׁ־יְהוָה וַתֹּאכַל אֶת־הָעֹלָה
וְאֶת־הָעֵצִים וְאֶת־הָאֲבָנִים וְאֶת־הֶעָפָר
וְאֶת־הַמַּיִם אֲשֶׁר־בַּתְּעָלָה לִחֵכָה:

18 <u>38</u> Then the fire of Yehovah fell, and consumed the burnt-offering, and the wood, and the stones, and the dust, and licked up the water that was in the trench.

לט וַיַּרְא כָּל־הָעָם וַיִּפְּלוּ עַל־פְּנֵיהֶם וַיֹּאמְרוּ
יְהוָה הוּא הָאֱלֹהִים יְהוָה הוּא הָאֱלֹהִים:

<u>39</u> And when all the people saw it, they fell on their faces; and they said: 'Yehovah, He is God; Yehovah, He is God.'
[1 Kings 18:38–39 The Pill Tanakh]

Having had any experience which helps to turn or return one to acknowledgement and trust in יְהוָה Yehovah is no doubt a good place to start one's continued journey in this life!

I said, **turn** or **return to** יְהוָה Yehovah as I know some folks have never had a relationship with the Almighty God, although many believe they have had such in the past.

For those who have been influenced by Christian doctrine (as in the Western world of our day), as I understand them, so many have concluded that they have nothing to **repent of,** perhaps because in professing *Jesus* they have come to believe that their past, present and future sins continue to be atoned for by Jesus!

However, <u>if</u> <u>they</u> <u>do</u> <u>not</u> <u>repent</u> <u>and</u> <u>do</u> <u>not</u> <u>live</u> <u>by</u> <u>the</u> <u>clear</u> <u>instructions</u> <u>written</u> <u>in</u> <u>the</u> <u>Torah</u> of יְהוָה **Yehovah, <u>then</u> <u>at</u> <u>the</u> <u>judgment</u> <u>when</u> <u>they</u> <u>come</u> <u>into</u> <u>the</u> <u>presence</u> <u>of</u> <u>the</u> <u>Almighty</u> God <u>will</u> <u>they</u> <u>be</u> <u>able</u> <u>to</u> <u>stand</u> (Daniel 12:1-2)?** By their attitudes, many think so! It appears that they believe that they don't have to do anything over and above what they currently do in order to come into the presence of Almighty God!

I believe it is unfortunate that **their doctrine puts a greater emphasis on how one thinks rather than on how one acts!**

Regardless of one's religious background, **the written Torah** (also known as the first five books in the Hebrew–language based Jewish Scriptures) **itself provides answers to having a sincere relationship with the Almighty God.**

30 11   For this commandment which I command thee this day, it is not too hard for thee, neither is it far off. [Deuteronomy 30:11 The Pill Tanakh]

יא כִּי הַמִּצְוָה הַזֹּאת אֲשֶׁר אָנֹכִי מְצַוְּךָ הַיּוֹם לֹא־נִפְלֵאת הִוא מִמְּךָ וְלֹא רְחֹקָה הִוא:

30 11 For this commandment which I command thee this day, it is not too hard for thee, neither is it far off.

יב לֹא בַשָּׁמַיִם הִוא לֵאמֹר מִי יַעֲלֶה־לָּנוּ הַשָּׁמַיְמָה וְיִקָּחֶהָ לָּנוּ וְיַשְׁמִעֵנוּ אֹתָהּ וְנַעֲשֶׂנָּה:

12 It is not in heaven, that thou shouldest say: 'Who shall go up for us to heaven, and bring it unto us, and make us to hear it, that we may do it?'

יג וְלֹא־מֵעֵבֶר לַיָּם הִוא לֵאמֹר מִי יַעֲבָר־לָנוּ אֶל־עֵבֶר הַיָּם וְיִקָּחֶהָ לָּנוּ וְיַשְׁמִעֵנוּ אֹתָהּ וְנַעֲשֶׂנָּה:

13 Neither is it beyond the sea, that thou shouldest say: 'Who shall go over the sea for us, and bring it unto us, and make us to hear it, that we may do it?'

יד כִּי־קָרוֹב אֵלֶיךָ הַדָּבָר מְאֹד בְּפִיךָ וּבִלְבָבְךָ לַעֲשֹׂתוֹ:

14 But the word is very nigh unto thee, in thy mouth, and in thy heart, that thou mayest do it.

טו רְאֵה נָתַתִּי לְפָנֶיךָ הַיּוֹם אֶת־הַחַיִּים וְאֶת־הַטּוֹב וְאֶת־הַמָּוֶת וְאֶת־הָרָע:

15 See, I have set before thee this day life and good, and death and evil,

יַ אֲשֶׁ֨ר אָנֹכִ֣י מְצַוְּךָ֮ הַיּוֹם֒ לְאַהֲבָ֞ה אֶת־יְהֹוָ֤ה אֱלֹהֶ֙יךָ֙ לָלֶ֣כֶת בִּדְרָכָ֔יו וְלִשְׁמֹ֛ר מִצְוֺתָ֥יו וְחֻקֹּתָ֖יו וּמִשְׁפָּטָ֑יו וְחָיִ֣יתָ וְרָבִ֔יתָ וּבֵרַכְךָ֙ יְהֹוָ֣ה אֱלֹהֶ֔יךָ בָּאָ֕רֶץ אֲשֶׁר־אַתָּ֥ה בָא־שָׁ֖מָּה לְרִשְׁתָּֽהּ׃

16 in that I command thee this day to love Yehovah thy God, to walk in His ways, and to keep His commandments and His statutes and His ordinances; then thou shalt live and multiply, and Yehovah thy God shall bless thee in the land whither thou goest in to possess it.

יַ וְאִם־יִפְנֶ֥ה לְבָבְךָ֖ וְלֹ֣א תִשְׁמָ֑ע וְנִדַּחְתָּ֗ וְהִשְׁתַּחֲוִ֛יתָ לֵאלֹהִ֥ים אֲחֵרִ֖ים וַעֲבַדְתָּֽם׃

17 But if thy heart turn away, and thou wilt not hear, but shalt be drawn away, and worship other gods, and serve them;

יַ הִגַּ֤דְתִּי לָכֶם֙ הַיּ֔וֹם כִּ֥י אָבֹ֖ד תֹּאבֵד֑וּן לֹא־תַאֲרִיכֻ֤ן יָמִים֙ עַל־הָ֣אֲדָמָ֔ה אֲשֶׁ֨ר אַתָּ֤ה עֹבֵר֙ אֶת־הַיַּרְדֵּ֔ן לָבֹ֥א שָׁ֖מָּה לְרִשְׁתָּֽהּ׃

18 I declare unto you this day, that ye shall surely perish; ye shall not prolong your days upon the land, whither thou passest over the Jordan to go in to possess it.

יַ הַעִדֹ֨תִי בָכֶ֣ם הַיּוֹם֮ אֶת־הַשָּׁמַ֣יִם וְאֶת־הָאָ֒רֶץ֒ הַחַיִּ֤ים וְהַמָּ֙וֶת֙ נָתַ֣תִּי לְפָנֶ֔יךָ הַבְּרָכָ֖ה וְהַקְּלָלָ֑ה וּבָֽחַרְתָּ֙ בַּֽחַיִּ֔ים לְמַ֥עַן תִּֽחְיֶ֖ה אַתָּ֥ה וְזַרְעֶֽךָ׃

19 I call heaven and earth to witness against you this day, that I have set before thee life and death, the blessing and the curse; therefore choose life, that thou mayest live, thou and thy seed;

כ לְאַהֲבָה֙ אֶת־יְהוָ֣ה אֱלֹהֶ֔יךָ לִשְׁמֹ֥עַ בְּקֹל֖וֹ וּלְדָבְקָה־ב֑וֹ
כִּ֣י ה֤וּא חַיֶּ֨יךָ֙ וְאֹ֣רֶךְ יָמֶ֔יךָ לָשֶׁ֣בֶת עַל־הָאֲדָמָ֗ה אֲשֶׁר֩ נִשְׁבַּ֨ע
יְהוָ֧ה לַאֲבֹתֶ֛יךָ לְאַבְרָהָ֥ם לְיִצְחָ֖ק וּֽלְיַעֲקֹ֑ב לָתֵ֥ת לָהֶֽם׃

20 to love Yehovah thy God, to hearken to His voice,
and to cleave unto Him; for that is thy life, and the
length of thy days; that thou mayest dwell in the land
which Yehovah swore unto thy fathers, to Abraham,
to Isaac, and to Jacob, to give them.
[Deuteronomy 30:11–20 The Pill Tanakh]

ל יה רְאֵ֨ה נָתַ֤תִּי לְפָנֶ֨יךָ֙ הַיּ֔וֹם אֶת־הַֽחַיִּ֖ים
וְאֶת־הַטּ֑וֹב וְאֶת־הַמָּ֖וֶת וְאֶת־הָרָֽע׃

30 15 **See, I have set before thee this day
life and good, and death and evil,**

יו אֲשֶׁ֣ר אָנֹכִ֣י מְצַוְּךָ֮ הַיּוֹם֒ לְאַהֲבָ֞ה אֶת־יְהוָ֣ה
אֱלֹהֶ֨יךָ֙ לָלֶ֣כֶת בִּדְרָכָ֔יו וְלִשְׁמֹ֛ר מִצְוֹתָ֥יו וְחֻקֹּתָ֖יו
וּמִשְׁפָּטָ֑יו וְחָיִ֣יתָ וְרָבִ֔יתָ וּבֵרַכְךָ֙ יְהוָ֣ה אֱלֹהֶ֔יךָ
בָּאָ֕רֶץ אֲשֶׁר־אַתָּ֥ה בָא־שָׁ֖מָּה לְרִשְׁתָּֽהּ׃

16 **in that I command thee this day to love
Yehovah thy God, to walk in His ways,
and to keep His commandments and His
statutes and His ordinances; then thou
shalt live and multiply, and Yehovah thy
God shall bless thee in the land whither
thou goest in to possess it.**
[Deuteronomy 30:15–16 The Pill Tanakh]

**How does one come to know about the commandments,
statutes and ordinances which are supposed to be kept?** The
obvious answer, to me, is by a discipline of reading the Jewish
Scriptures on a regular basis!

I highly recommend for anyone who is interested in improving their relationship with the Almighty God to take on the discipline of a Scripture reading plan that will help provide a framework for you to read it in its entirety through each year.[1]

Moreover, for any of you who are not familiar with the ancient Hebrew language as found in the handwritten Leningrad Codex, I would encourage you to begin the process of learning to read and understand it!

גּ ט כִּי־אָז אֶהְפֹּךְ אֶל־עַמִּים שָׂפָה
בְרוּרָה לִקְרֹא כֻלָּם בְּשֵׁם יְהֹוָה
לְעָבְדוֹ שְׁכֶם אֶחָד׃

3 9 For then will I turn to the peoples a pure language, that they may all call upon the name of Yehovah, to serve Him with one consent. [Zephaniah 3:9 The Pill Tanakh]

If you are unfamiliar with the Hebrew language, I am including a couple of charts which may introduce you to Hebrew! Below, please find the following charts, first the Hebrew letters, followed by vowel pointers and a brief introduction to Hebrew Cantillation. It is my hope that you come to recognize Hebrew letters and vowels as a starting place to facilitate a study of Biblical Hebrew!

---

[1] The following are two internet sources for reading the Scriptures daily throughout the year.
Leningrad Codex Hebrew Modified JPS 1917 English Daily Readings, online at
https://www.the-iconoclast.org/resources/daily/read_Tanakh.php.
Downloadable Pdf 'Read Scripture In–A–Year!' can be found online at
http://sarshalom.us/resources/scripture/read_scripture-in-a-year.pdf.

HEBREW LETTERS

LETTER	NAME	PRONUNCIATION
א	Aleph	Orig. the glottal stop. Now silent in the middle of words if it has no vowel; otherwise it is pronounced according to the accompanying vowel sign.
בּ	Bet	**b**
ב	Vet	**bh, v**
גּ	Gimel	Pronounced like **g** in **get**
ג	Gimel	Orig. pronounced – with a slight aspiration of the sound – like **gh.**
דּ	Dalet	**d**
ד	Dalet	Orig. pronounced like **th** in **this.**
ה	He	**h**
ו	Vav	**v**
ז	Zayin	**z**
ח	Het	Pronounced like **ch** in Scot. **loch.** It is a guttural sound made in the back of the throat.
ט	Tet	An emphatic **t**
י	Yod	**y**

LETTER	NAME	PRONUNCIATION
כ	Kaph	k
ך	Kaph Sofit	k (at end of a word)
כ	Khaph	kh
ך	Khaph Sofit	kh (at end of a word)
ל	Lamed	l
מ	Mem	m
ם	Mem Sofit	m (at end of a word)
נ	Nun	n
ן	Nun Sofit	n (at end of a word)
ס	Samekh	s
ע	Ayin	A strong guttural sound, like a deep *aw.*
פ	Pe	p
פ	Phe	f
ף	Phe Sofit	f (at end of a word)
צ	Tzade	tz – Occasionally pronounced like an emphatic *s.*
ץ	Tzade Sofit	tz – Occasionally pronounced like an emphatic *s* (at end of a word).

LETTER	NAME	PRONUNCIATION
ק	Quf	an emphatic **k.**
ר	Resh	**r** (like a Spanish **rolled or trilled 'r'** (rolled with tongue). In the Hebrew the sound is made with a **rolling/trilling** vibration in back of the throat).
שׁ	Shin	**sh** (Shin is designated with a **dot at the upper right** of the character).
שׂ	Sin	**s** (Sin is designated with a **dot at the upper left** of the character).
תּ	Taw, Tav	**t** or hard **'th'.**
ת	Thaw, Thav	Orig. pronounced like **th** in **thing.**

HEBREW VOWEL CHART

VOWEL	NAME	PRONUNCIATION
אָ	KAMATZ – קָמָץ	**AH** long vowel; as the *'a'* in *father*.
אֳ	HATAF KAMATZ – חֲטָף קָמָץ	**AH** reduced long vowel; like *o* in *gone;* a schwa sound, with just a hint of the *aw* as in *saw.*
אַ	PATACH – פַּתַח	**AH, UH** short vowel sound; like *a* in *father* or *a* as in *was.*
אֲ	HATAF PATACH – חֲטָף פַּתַח	**AH, UH** reduced vowel; a *schwa* sound, with just a hint of the *e* as in *met.*
אֶ	SEGOL – סֶגּוֹל	**EH** short vowel; like the *e* as in *met.*
אֱ	HATAF SEGOL – חֲטָף סֶגּוֹל	**EH** reduced vowel; a *schwa* sound, with just a hint of the *e* as in *met.*
בְ	SHEVA – שְׁוָא	**EH** vowel or STOP; at the end of a syllable: silent; in middle of syllable: a *schwa* sound, *a* as in *alone.*
אִ	HIRIQ – חִירִיק	**EE** short vowel; *i* as in *machine.*

VOWEL	NAME	PRONUNCIATION
אִי	HIRIQ MALAY– חִירִיק מָלֵא	**EE** short vowel.
לֹ	CHOLAM CHASER– חֹלָם חָסֵר	**OH** long vowel; like the **o** in the word **alone.** The dot is to the upper left of the letter (with the Lamed, to the left of the upper stem, with other letters like the HET, it appears at the above left [חֹ]).
וֹ	CHOLAM MALAY– חֹלָם מָלֵא	**OH** long vowel.
וּ	SHURUK – שׁוּרוּק	**OO** long vowel; like **oo** in the word **moon.** The Shuruk is always [וּ] the Vav (right) with the dagesh (left).
אֻ	KUBUTZ – קֻבּוּץ	**OO** short vowel; like **oo** in the word **moon.** The Kubutz is the three dots, beginning under the left side of the Hebrew letter, and proceeding diagonally down to the right.
אֵ	TSERE – צֵרֵי	**AY** long vowel; like the **ey** in the word **they.**

Hebrew Cantillation

DISJUNCTIVES (separating) AND CONJUNCTIVES (joining)

"The Hebrew Bible is punctuated with an elaborate system of stylized inflections that delineate the most subtle nuances of meaning.   For centuries this system was a purely oral tradition.   Only the consonantal text was written down: the inflection had to be memorized. By the seventh century, the rabbis who considered themselves guardians of the sacred text became concerned that the correct melodic inflections were in danger of being forgotten. They therefore devised a set of symbols that would punctuate the text and indicate the proper motif to which each and every word was to be chanted. The *ta'amey ha-mikra* do more than merely indicate which syllable of each word is to be accented. For that function alone, one symbol would have been enough. not thirty. The *Te'amim* function as an elaborate punctuation system. a means of parsing the syntax of classical Hebrew. ...."

"On the page we could resolve the [accent] ambiguity if we had some form of detailed punctuation indicating which words are connected and which words are separated by a pause."

"The Masoretic system provides just such a system. There are two basic types of punctuation marks:"

● **"disjunctive accents,"** which indicate a pause or separation.
● **"conjunctive accents,"**   which indicate a connection.[2]

---

[2]Joshua R. Jacobson, 'Chanting the Hebrew Bible', (Jewish Publication Society, Philadelphia, Copyright 2002), p23.

Five Levels Of Hebrew Cantillation

1) Level 1, known as the *Emperor Level.* Only two accents [cantillation marks] are in this category:

    a) *Ethnacta,* with some exceptions, **expresses the logical end of the first half of a longer verse;** and

    b) *Silluk,* **which is found in the last word of each and every verse in the Hebrew text of the Jewish Bible!**

2) Level 2, known as the *King Level.*
3) Level 3, known as the *Duke Level.*
4) Level 4, known as the *Count Level.*
5) Level 5, known as the *Servant Level.*

This introduction to Hebrew cantillation is very rudimentary. For a complete discussion I refer you to the book by Joshua Jacobson[3] or my web page devoted to Hebrew Letters, Vowels and Cantillation.[4]

In this chapter I started with a passage from Isaiah 55:6, *Seek ye Yehovah while He may be found.* I followed with a discussion on repentance, which is based upon having a relationship with Yehovah by returning to Him with humility. I discussed having a Scripture reading plan to help bring about a greater foundation to that relationship.

I began the end of the chapter with the iconic passage from Zephaniah 3:9 which speaks about turning peoples to a pure language (the Hebrew language being inferred).

Knowledge of the ancient Hebrew is critical in understanding the Hebrew text. Thus, I provided information introducing the Hebrew letters, followed by Hebrew vowels and cantillation.

---

[3] ibid
[4] My web page dealing with Hebrew Letters, Vowels and Cantillation is https://www.the-iconoclast.org/reference/HebrewLettersVowelsAccents.php

מַלְכוּת הַשָּׁמַיִם
The Kingdom Of Heaven

Few topics illicit a storm of emotion as much as מַלְכוּת הַשָּׁמַיִם —
The Kingdom Of Heaven.   Since early on in the history of the
world, the idea of heaven has captivated the hearts and minds of
many people. Mankind's efforts to reach beyond the bounds of their
terrestrial limits is found in the account of **The Tower of Babel.**

יא א וַיְהִי כָל־הָאָרֶץ שָׂפָה אֶחָת וּדְבָרִים
אֲחָדִים:

11 1   And the whole earth was of one
language and of one speech.

ב וַיְהִי בְּנָסְעָם מִקֶּדֶם וַיִּמְצְאוּ בִקְעָה בְּאֶרֶץ שִׁנְעָר
וַיֵּשְׁבוּ שָׁם:

2 And it came to pass, as they journeyed east,
that they found a plain in the land of Shinar;
and they dwelt there.

ג וַיֹּאמְרוּ אִישׁ אֶל־רֵעֵהוּ הָבָה נִלְבְּנָה לְבֵנִים
וְנִשְׂרְפָה לִשְׂרֵפָה וַתְּהִי לָהֶם הַלְּבֵנָה לְאָבֶן
וְהַחֵמָר הָיָה לָהֶם לַחֹמֶר:

3 And they said one to another: 'Come, let us
make brick, and burn them thoroughly.' And
they had brick for stone, and slime had they
for mortar.

ד וַיֹּאמְרוּ הָבָה | נִבְנֶה־לָּנוּ עִיר וּמִגְדָּל וְרֹאשׁוֹ
בַשָּׁמַיִם וְנַעֲשֶׂה־לָּנוּ שֵׁם פֶּן־נָפוּץ עַל־פְּנֵי
כָל־הָאָרֶץ:

4 And they said: 'Come, let us build us a city,
and a tower, with its top in heaven, and let us
make us a name; lest we be scattered abroad
upon the face of the whole earth.'

ה וַיֵּרֶד יְהֹוָה לִרְאֹת אֶת־הָעִיר וְאֶת־הַמִּגְדָּל אֲשֶׁר בָּנוּ בְּנֵי הָאָדָם:

5 And Yehovah came down to see the city and the tower, which the children of men builded.

ו וַיֹּאמֶר יְהֹוָה הֵן עַם אֶחָד וְשָׂפָה אַחַת לְכֻלָּם וְזֶה הַחִלָּם לַעֲשׂוֹת וְעַתָּה לֹא־יִבָּצֵר מֵהֶם כֹּל אֲשֶׁר יָזְמוּ לַעֲשׂוֹת:

6 And Yehovah said: 'Behold, they are one people, and they have all one language; and this is what they begin to do; and now nothing will be withholden from them, which they purpose to do.

ז הָבָה נֵרְדָה וְנָבְלָה שָׁם שְׂפָתָם אֲשֶׁר לֹא יִשְׁמְעוּ אִישׁ שְׂפַת רֵעֵהוּ:

7 Come, let us go down, and there confound their language, that they may not understand one another's speech.'

ח וַיָּפֶץ יְהֹוָה אֹתָם מִשָּׁם עַל־פְּנֵי כָל־הָאָרֶץ וַיַּחְדְּלוּ לִבְנֹת הָעִיר:

8 So Yehovah scattered them abroad from thence upon the face of all the earth; and they left off to build the city.

ט עַל־כֵּן קָרָא שְׁמָהּ בָּבֶל כִּי־שָׁם בָּלַל יְהֹוָה שְׂפַת כָּל־הָאָרֶץ וּמִשָּׁם הֱפִיצָם יְהֹוָה עַל־פְּנֵי כָּל־הָאָרֶץ:

9 Therefore was the name of it called Babel; because Yehovah did there confound the language of all the earth; and from thence did Yehovah scatter them abroad upon the face of all the earth. [Genesis 11:1-9 The Pill Tanakh]

4 And they said: 'Come, let us build us a city, and a tower, with its top in heaven, and let us make us a name; lest we be scattered abroad upon the face of the whole earth.'

The story of the Tower of Babel illustrates an effort of the people to reach to the heavens by building a tower "with its top in heaven."

The fact is that Heaven is above the earth.   It is in a different realm.   Mankind was made terrestrial, to live on earth.   Yet, to acknowledge the majesty of Yehovah, whose domain is exclusively in the heavens, was even at issue at the early time in the attempt to build a tower with its top in heaven.

Quite obviously, they were trying to gain access to Heaven **without repentance and without seeking Yehovah with all of their heart, soul and might** (Deuteronomy 6:5).

The prophet Isaiah captured the magnificent greatness of the separation of Yehovah over His creation in chapter 55.

סֹה ‎6 דִּרְשׁוּ יְהוָה בְּהִמָּצְאוֹ קְרָאֻהוּ בִּהְיוֹתוֹ
קָרוֹב:

55 6 Seek ye Yehovah while He may be found, call ye upon Him while He is near;

‎7 יַעֲזֹב רָשָׁע דַּרְכּוֹ וְאִישׁ אָוֶן מַחְשְׁבֹתָיו וְיָשֹׁב
אֶל־יְהוָה וִירַחֲמֵהוּ וְאֶל־אֱלֹהֵינוּ כִּי־יַרְבֶּה
לִסְלוֹחַ:

7 Let the wicked forsake his way, and the man of iniquity his thoughts; and let him return unto Yehovah, and He will have compassion upon him, and to our God, for He will abundantly pardon.

חַ יַעֲזֹב רָשָׁע דַּרְכּוֹ וְאִישׁ אָוֶן מַחְשְׁבֹתָיו וְיָשֹׁב
אֶל־יְהוָה וִירַחֲמֵהוּ וְאֶל־אֱלֹהֵינוּ כִּי־יַרְבֶּה
לִסְלוֹחַ:

8 For My thoughts are not your thoughts, neither are your ways My ways, saith Yehovah.

ט כִּי לֹא מַחְשְׁבוֹתַי מַחְשְׁבוֹתֵיכֶם וְלֹא דַרְכֵיכֶם
דְּרָכָי נְאֻם יְהוָה:

9 For as the heavens are higher than the earth, so are My ways higher than your ways, and My thoughts than your thoughts. [Isaiah 55:6-9 The Pill Tanakh]

It is evident that Isaiah was concerned with showing that Yehovah, the creator of the universe, is far above mankind not only in space, but also in wisdom, knowledge, thought and understanding.

The Kingdom of Heaven מַלְכוּת הַשָּׁמַיִם is higher than the earth!

Below are a couple of quotes regarding the Kingdom of Heaven from Jewish sources:

Belief in Heaven is Fundamental to Judaism

I am often asked by Jews and non-Jews to explain the Jewish view of heaven and hell. A few prefatory remarks will help guide us on our exploration and understanding of this seemingly obscure concept. In this post we try to answer the question - Does Judaism Believe in Heaven and Hell? Is there a Jewish heaven?

Biblical Sources

The Torah says, *"and the Almighty formed man of dust from the earth, and He blew into his nostrils the SOUL of life"* **(Genesis 2:7)** . Human beings are composed of two aspects: The physical body which is formed from the dust of the earth and the spiritual soul (our real essence) which is directly from God. This is why the soul is described by King Solomon as, *"The candle of God is the soul of man"* **(Proverbs 20:27)** . The soul is a part of God, pure and unblemished.

The body does serve an important purpose. It enables us (our souls) to live a life in this physical world. This presents us with the unique opportunity to serve God by following His divine game plan as outlined in the Torah. Following God's will by fulfilling His commandments in this physical world connects us to God spiritually (the root of the Hebrew word *"mitzvah"* is *"tzavta"* which literally means *"to connect"*), refines the physical world, and proclaims the glory of God — that He exists everywhere. This is our mission while on earth.

Quotes of King Solomon

At death the soul and body separate. King Solomon said, *"The dust will return to the ground as it was, and the spirit will return to God who gave it"* **(Ecclesiastes 12:7**). This means the soul returns to heaven, back to God, where it is enveloped in the Oneness of the Divine.

Solomon also said there is an *"advantage of light over darkness"* **(Ecclesiastes 2:13**). This means that when a person perseveres and serves God in a world full of darkness, the soul is rewarded with an enhanced sensitivity to appreciate Godliness. In heaven the soul experiences the greatest possible pleasure—a greater perception and feeling of closeness to God than it had previously.

Although Judaism believes in heaven, the Torah

speaks very little about it. The Torah focuses less on how we get to heaven and considerably more on how to live our lives. We perform the mitzvot because it is our privilege and our sacred obligation to do so. We perform them out of a sense of love and duty, not out of a desire to get something in return. There is a practical reason for this. If we lived a righteous life for the sake of a monetary or heavenly reward it would be serving God for an ulterior motive.[1]

...

What is the Kingdom of Heaven?

The "Kingdom of Heaven" (מַלְכוּת הַשָּׁמַיִם, *malchut hashamaim*) is an ancient Jewish idea easily traced back to the Hebrew Bible, where the prophets speak of a coming messianic age when God will establish His kingdom on earth. Isaiah prophesied that "the government will be upon" Messiah's shoulder "and His name will be called Wonderful Counselor, Mighty God, Everlasting Father, Prince of Peace" (Isaiah 9:6). In reality, God was always supposed to be the king (מֶלֶךְ, *melech*) of Israel, but in 1 Sam 8:7, he says to Samuel, his servant, "they have rejected Me from being King over them." A sad state of affairs. Yet many Hebrew prophets still look to the day when Israel and the whole world will be ruled by Hashem himself, "And the YHVH (יהוה, *Adonai*) will be King over all the earth; on that day the Lord will be the only one, and His name the only one" (Zech 14:19).

The kingdom (מַלְכוּת, *malchut*) must have a proper ruler (מֶלֶךְ, *melech*). In Jewish thinking, this sovereign reign of God on earth is understood as the

---

[1] Guest Author, 'Belief in Heaven is Fundamental to Judaism,' Jews for Judaism, accessed 4 Nov 2025, https://jewsforjudaism.org/knowledge/articles/belief-in-heaven-is-fundamental-to-judaism.

future. The LORD (יהוה, *Adonai*) will be king. And yet a measure of this spiritual reality of God's reign can be experienced at any moment, and that is the broader idea of the "Kingdom of Heaven" (מַלְכוּת הַשָּׁמַיִם, *malchut hashamaim*) we encounter on the pages of the Jewish gospels in particular.[2]

In Jewish thinking, this sovereign reign of God on earth is understood as the future. The LORD (יהוה, *Adonai*) will be king.

There is, also, a relatively obscure passage in the last chapter of Daniel which gives a *sense of everlasting life and ultimate judgment,* where actions of man are accounted for!

12 1 And at that time shall Michael stand up, the great prince who standeth for the children of thy people; and there shall be a time of trouble, such as never was since there was a nation even to that same time; and at that time thy people shall be delivered, every one that shall be found written in the book.

2 And many of them that sleep in the dust of the earth shall awake, some to everlasting life, and some to reproaches and everlasting abhorrence.

3 And they that are wise shall shine as the brightness of the firmament; and they that turn the many to righteousness as the stars for ever and ever.

[Daniel 12:1-3 The Pill Tanakh]

---

[2]Pinchas Shir, 'What is the Kingdom of Heaven,' last updated 21 Feb 2024, https://www.pshir.com/what-is-the-kingdom-of-heaven/.

10 14   Behold, unto Yehovah thy God belongeth the heaven, and the heaven of heavens, the earth, with all that therein is.

[Deuteronomy 10:14 The Pill Tanakh]

יֵב וְעַתָּה֙ יִשְׂרָאֵ֔ל מָ֚ה יְהוָ֣ה אֱלֹהֶ֔יךָ שֹׁאֵ֖ל מֵעִמָּ֑ךְ כִּ֣י
אִם־לְ֠יִרְאָה אֶת־יְהוָ֨ה אֱלֹהֶ֜יךָ לָלֶ֣כֶת בְּכָל־דְּרָכָיו֙
וּלְאַהֲבָ֣ה אֹת֔וֹ וְלַעֲבֹד֙ אֶת־יְהוָ֣ה אֱלֹהֶ֔יךָ בְּכָל־לְבָבְךָ֖
וּבְכָל־נַפְשֶֽׁךָ׃

10 12   And now, Israel, what doth Yehovah thy God require of thee, but to fear Yehovah thy God, to walk in all His ways, and to love Him, and to serve Yehovah thy God with all thy heart and with all thy soul;

יֵג לִשְׁמֹ֞ר אֶת־מִצְוֺ֤ת יְהוָה֙ וְאֶת־חֻקֹּתָ֔יו אֲשֶׁ֛ר אָנֹכִ֥י מְצַוְּךָ֖
הַיּ֑וֹם לְט֖וֹב לָֽךְ׃

13   to keep the commandments of Yehovah, and His statutes, which I command thee this day, for thy good?

יֵד הֵ֚ן לַיהוָ֣ה אֱלֹהֶ֔יךָ הַשָּׁמַ֖יִם וּשְׁמֵ֣י הַשָּׁמָ֑יִם הָאָ֖רֶץ
וְכָל־אֲשֶׁר־בָּֽהּ׃

14   Behold, unto Yehovah thy God belongeth the heaven, and the heaven of heavens, the earth, with all that therein is.

יֵה רַ֧ק בַּאֲבֹתֶ֛יךָ חָשַׁ֥ק יְהוָ֖ה לְאַהֲבָ֣ה אוֹתָ֑ם וַיִּבְחַ֞ר
בְּזַרְעָ֣ם אַחֲרֵיהֶ֗ם בָּכֶ֛ם מִכָּל־הָעַמִּ֖ים כַּיּ֥וֹם הַזֶּֽה׃

15   Only Yehovah had a delight in thy fathers to love them, and He chose their seed after them, even you, above all peoples, as it is this day.

יֵ וּמַלְתֶּם אֵת עָרְלַת לְבַבְכֶם וְעָרְפְּכֶם לֹא תַקְשׁוּ עוֹד :

16 Circumcise therefore the foreskin of your heart, and be no more stiffnecked.

יֵ כִּי יְהוָה אֱלֹהֵיכֶם הוּא אֱלֹהֵי הָאֱלֹהִים וַאֲדֹנֵי הָאֲדֹנִים הָאֵל הַגָּדֹל הַגִּבֹּר וְהַנּוֹרָא אֲשֶׁר לֹא־יִשָּׂא פָנִים וְלֹא יִקַּח שֹׁחַד :

17 For Yehovah your God, He is God of gods, and Lord of lords, the great God, the mighty, and the awful, who regardeth not persons, nor taketh reward.

יֵח עֹשֶׂה מִשְׁפַּט יָתוֹם וְאַלְמָנָה וְאֹהֵב גֵּר לָתֶת לוֹ לֶחֶם וְשִׂמְלָה :

18 He doth execute justice for the fatherless and widow, and loveth the stranger, in giving him food and raiment.

יֵט וַאֲהַבְתֶּם אֶת־הַגֵּר כִּי־גֵרִים הֱיִיתֶם בְּאֶרֶץ מִצְרָיִם :

19 Love ye therefore the stranger; for ye were strangers in the land of Egypt.

כ אֶת־יְהוָה אֱלֹהֶיךָ תִּירָא אֹתוֹ תַעֲבֹד וּבוֹ תִדְבָּק וּבִשְׁמוֹ תִּשָּׁבֵעַ :

20 Thou shalt fear Yehovah thy God; Him shalt thou serve; and to Him shalt thou cleave, and by His name shalt thou swear.

כֵא הוּא תְהִלָּתְךָ וְהוּא אֱלֹהֶיךָ אֲשֶׁר־עָשָׂה אִתְּךָ אֶת־הַגְּדֹלֹת וְאֶת־הַנּוֹרָאֹת הָאֵלֶּה אֲשֶׁר רָאוּ עֵינֶיךָ :

21 He is thy glory, and He is thy God, that hath done for thee these great and tremendous things, which thine eyes have seen.

כב בְּשִׁבְעִים נֶפֶשׁ יָרְדוּ אֲבֹתֶיךָ מִצְרָיְמָה וְעַתָּה שָׂמְךָ יְהוָה אֱלֹהֶיךָ כְּכוֹכְבֵי הַשָּׁמַיִם לָרֹב:

<u>22</u> With seventy persons thy fathers went down into Egypt; and now Yehovah thy God hath made thee as the stars of heaven for multitude.
[Deuteronomy 10:12-22 The Pill Tanakh]

---

10 <u>16</u> Circumcise therefore the foreskin of your heart, and be no more stiffnecked.

<u>17</u> For Yehovah your God, He is God of gods, and Lord of lords, the great God, the mighty, and the awful, who regardeth not persons, nor taketh reward.
[Deuteronomy 10:16-17 The Pill Tanakh]

The ancient Jewish Scriptures are replete with passages which declare the greatness of Yehovah, and which direct His people to worship Him by observing His statutes, ordinances and commandments and to love Him with all their heart and with all their soul.

When we, as a people whose domain is the created earth, acknowledge that Yehovah is holy, reigning in His domain of Heaven, **how can we not but worship Him alone?**

10 <u>14</u> Behold, unto Yehovah thy God belongeth the heaven, and the heaven of heavens, the earth, with all that therein is.
[Deuteronomy 10:14 The Pill Tanakh]

The End Of The Matter

י **יד** הֵן לַיהוָה אֱלֹהֶיךָ הַשָּׁמַיִם וּשְׁמֵי
הַשָּׁמָיִם הָאָרֶץ וְכָל־אֲשֶׁר־בָּהּ:

10 <u>14</u> Behold, unto Yehovah thy God belongeth the heaven, and the heaven of heavens, the earth, with all that therein is.

כ אֶת־יְהוָה אֱלֹהֶיךָ תִּירָא אֹתוֹ תַעֲבֹד וּבוֹ
תִדְבָּק וּבִשְׁמוֹ תִּשָּׁבֵעַ:

<u>20</u> Thou shalt fear Yehovah thy God; Him shalt thou serve; and to Him shalt thou cleave, and by His name shalt thou swear.

כא הוּא תְהִלָּתְךָ וְהוּא אֱלֹהֶיךָ אֲשֶׁר־עָשָׂה
אִתְּךָ אֶת־הַגְּדֹלֹת וְאֶת־הַנּוֹרָאֹת הָאֵלֶּה
אֲשֶׁר רָאוּ עֵינֶיךָ:

<u>21</u> He is thy glory, and He is thy God, that hath done for thee these great and tremendous things, which thine eyes have seen. [Deuteronomy 10:14, 20-21 The Pill Tanakh]

The *Beginning* And End Of The Matter is <u>14</u> *Behold, unto Yehovah thy God belongeth the heaven, and the heaven of heavens, the earth, with all that therein is.*

The fact is that יְהוָה **Yehovah is the Almighty God!** He dwells in Heaven, even the heaven of heavens; and we, the people, dwell below, on the earth!

<u>20</u> **Thou shalt fear Yehovah thy God; Him shalt thou serve; and to Him shalt thou cleave, and by His name shalt thou swear.** <u>21</u> **He is thy glory, and He is thy God,**

**that hath done for thee these great and tremendous
things, which thine eyes have seen.**

What is known as the "Central Prayer of Judaism," **The Sh'ma**
(Deuteronomy 6:4) succinctly proclaims these truths:

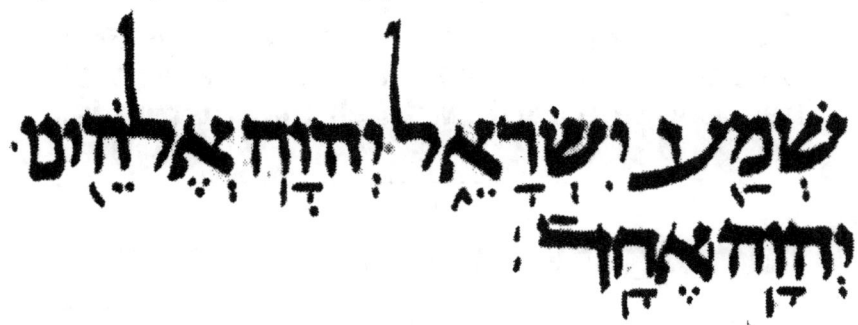

דַ שְׁמַע יִשְׂרָאֵל יְהֹוָה אֱלֹהֵינוּ יְהֹוָה ׀ אֶחָד:

<u>4</u> Hear, O Israel: Yehovah our God, Yehovah is one.

The Sh'ma can best be understood within its context!

Deuteronomy 6:1-25

ו א וְזֹאת הַמִּצְוָה הַחֻקִּים וְהַמִּשְׁפָּטִים אֲשֶׁר צִוָּה
יְהֹוָה אֱלֹהֵיכֶם לְלַמֵּד אֶתְכֶם לַעֲשׂוֹת בָּאָרֶץ אֲשֶׁר
אַתֶּם עֹבְרִים שָׁמָּה לְרִשְׁתָּהּ:

6 <u>1</u> Now this is the commandment, the
statutes, and the ordinances, which Yehovah
your God commanded to teach you, that ye
might do them in the l and whither ye go over
to possess it--

ב לְמַעַן תִּירָא אֶת־יְהֹוָה אֱלֹהֶיךָ לִשְׁמֹר
אֶת־כָּל־חֻקֹּתָיו וּמִצְוֹתָיו אֲשֶׁר אָנֹכִי מְצַוְּךָ אַתָּה
וּבִנְךָ וּבֶן־בִּנְךָ כֹּל יְמֵי חַיֶּיךָ וּלְמַעַן יַאֲרִכֻן
יָמֶיךָ:

2 that thou mightest fear Yehovah thy God, to keep all His statutes and His commandments, which I command thee, thou, and thy son, and thy son's son, all the days of thy life; and that thy days may be prolonged.

גּ וְשָׁמַעְתָּ יִשְׂרָאֵל וְשָׁמַרְתָּ לַעֲשׂוֹת אֲשֶׁר יִיטַב לְךָ וַאֲשֶׁר תִּרְבּוּן מְאֹד כַּאֲשֶׁר דִּבֶּר יְהֹוָה אֱלֹהֵי אֲבֹתֶיךָ לָךְ אֶרֶץ זָבַת חָלָב וּדְבָשׁ:

3 Hear therefore, O Israel, and observe to do it; that it may be well with thee, and that ye may increase mightily, as Yehovah, the God of thy fathers, hath promised unto thee--a land flowing with milk and honey.

ד שְׁמַ**ע** יִשְׂרָאֵל יְהֹוָה אֱלֹהֵינוּ יְהֹוָה ׀ אֶחָ**ד**:

4 Hear, O Israel: Yehovah our God, Yehovah is one.

ה וְאָהַבְתָּ אֵת יְהֹוָה אֱלֹהֶיךָ בְּכָל־לְבָבְךָ וּבְכָל־נַפְשְׁךָ וּבְכָל־מְאֹדֶךָ:

5 And thou shalt love Yehovah thy God with all thy heart, and with all thy soul, and with all thy might.

ו וְהָיוּ הַדְּבָרִים הָאֵלֶּה אֲשֶׁר אָנֹכִי מְצַוְּךָ הַיּוֹם עַל־לְבָבֶךָ:

6 And these words, which I command thee this day, shall be upon thy heart;

ז וְשִׁנַּנְתָּם לְבָנֶיךָ וְדִבַּרְתָּ בָּם בְּשִׁבְתְּךָ בְּבֵיתֶךָ וּבְלֶכְתְּךָ בַדֶּרֶךְ וּבְשָׁכְבְּךָ וּבְקוּמֶךָ:

7 and thou shalt teach them diligently unto thy children, and shalt talk of them when thou sittest in thy house, and when thou walkest by

the way, and when thou liest down, and when thou risest up.

ח   וּקְשַׁרְתָּ֥ם לְא֖וֹת עַל־יָדֶ֑ךָ וְהָי֥וּ לְטֹטָפֹ֖ת בֵּ֥ין עֵינֶֽיךָ׃

8 And thou shalt bind them for a sign upon thy hand, and they shall be for frontlets between thine eyes.

ט   וּכְתַבְתָּ֛ם עַל־מְזוּזֹ֥ת בֵּיתֶ֖ךָ וּבִשְׁעָרֶֽיךָ׃

9   And thou shalt write them upon the door-posts of thy house, and upon thy gates.

י   וְהָיָ֞ה כִּ֥י יְבִֽיאֲךָ֣ ׀ יְהוָ֣ה אֱלֹהֶ֗יךָ אֶל־הָאָ֜רֶץ אֲשֶׁ֨ר נִשְׁבַּ֧ע לַאֲבֹתֶ֛יךָ לְאַבְרָהָ֥ם לְיִצְחָ֖ק וּֽלְיַעֲקֹ֑ב לָ֣תֶת לָ֑ךְ עָרִ֛ים גְּדֹלֹ֥ת וְטֹבֹ֖ת אֲשֶׁ֥ר לֹא־בָנִֽיתָ׃

10   And it shall be, when Yehovah thy God shall bring thee into the land which He swore unto thy fathers, to Abraham, to Isaac, and to Jacob, to give thee--great and goodly cities, which thou didst not build,

יא   וּבָתִּ֞ים מְלֵאִ֣ים כָּל־טוּב֮ אֲשֶׁ֣ר לֹא־מִלֵּאתָ֒ וּבֹרֹ֤ת חֲצוּבִים֙ אֲשֶׁ֣ר לֹא־חָצַ֔בְתָּ כְּרָמִ֥ים וְזֵיתִ֖ים אֲשֶׁ֣ר לֹא־נָטָ֑עְתָּ וְאָכַלְתָּ֖ וְשָׂבָֽעְתָּ׃

11   and houses full of all good things, which thou didst not fill, and cisterns hewn out, which thou didst not hew, vineyards and olive-trees, which thou didst not plant, and thou shalt eat and be satisfied--

יב   הִשָּׁ֣מֶר לְךָ֔ פֶּן־תִּשְׁכַּ֖ח אֶת־יְהוָ֑ה אֲשֶׁ֧ר הוֹצִֽיאֲךָ֛ מֵאֶ֥רֶץ מִצְרַ֖יִם מִבֵּ֥ית עֲבָדִֽים׃

12   then beware lest thou forget Yehovah, who brought thee forth out of the land of Egypt, out

of the house of bondage.

יג   אֶת־יְהוָה אֱלֹהֶיךָ תִּירָא וְאֹתוֹ תַעֲבֹד וּבִשְׁמוֹ
תִּשָּׁבֵעַ:

<u>13</u> Thou shalt fear Yehovah thy God; and Him shalt thou serve, and by His name shalt thou swear.

יד   לֹא תֵלְכוּן אַחֲרֵי אֱלֹהִים אֲחֵרִים מֵאֱלֹהֵי
הָעַמִּים אֲשֶׁר סְבִיבוֹתֵיכֶם:

<u>14</u> Ye shall not go after other gods, of the gods of the peoples that are round about you;

יה   כִּי אֵל קַנָּא יְהוָה אֱלֹהֶיךָ בְּקִרְבֶּךָ פֶּן־יֶחֱרֶה
אַף־יְהוָה אֱלֹהֶיךָ בָּךְ וְהִשְׁמִידְךָ מֵעַל פְּנֵי
הָאֲדָמָה:

<u>15</u> for a jealous God, even Yehovah thy God, is in the midst of thee; lest the anger of Yehovah thy God be kindled against thee, and He destroy thee from off the face of the earth.

יו   לֹא תְנַסּוּ אֶת־יְהוָה אֱלֹהֵיכֶם כַּאֲשֶׁר נִסִּיתֶם
בַּמַּסָּה:

<u>16</u> Ye shall not try Yehovah your God, as ye tried Him in Massah.

יז   שָׁמוֹר תִּשְׁמְרוּן אֶת־מִצְוֹת יְהוָה אֱלֹהֵיכֶם
וְעֵדֹתָיו וְחֻקָּיו אֲשֶׁר צִוָּךְ:

<u>17</u>   Ye   shall   diligently   keep   the commandments of Yehovah your God, and His testimonies, and His statutes, which He hath commanded thee.

יח   וְעָשִׂיתָ הַיָּשָׁר וְהַטּוֹב בְּעֵינֵי יְהוָה לְמַעַן יִיטַב
לָךְ וּבָאתָ וְיָרַשְׁתָּ אֶת־הָאָרֶץ הַטֹּבָה אֲשֶׁר־נִשְׁבַּע

יְהֹוָה לַאֲבֹתֶיךָ:

18 And thou shalt do that which is right and good in the sight of Yehovah; that it may be well with thee, and that thou mayest go in and possess the good land which Yehovah swore unto thy fathers,

יט לַהֲדֹף אֶת־כָּל־אֹיְבֶיךָ מִפָּנֶיךָ כַּאֲשֶׁר דִּבֶּר יְהֹוָה:

19 to thrust out all thine enemies from before thee, as Yehovah hath spoken.

כ כִּי־יִשְׁאָלְךָ בִנְךָ מָחָר לֵאמֹר מָה הָעֵדֹת וְהַחֻקִּים וְהַמִּשְׁפָּטִים אֲשֶׁר צִוָּה יְהֹוָה אֱלֹהֵינוּ אֶתְכֶם:

20 When thy son asketh thee in time to come, saying: 'What mean the testimonies, and the statutes, and the ordinances, which Yehovah our God hath commanded you?

כא וְאָמַרְתָּ לְבִנְךָ עֲבָדִים הָיִינוּ לְפַרְעֹה בְּמִצְרָיִם וַיּוֹצִיאֵנוּ יְהֹוָה מִמִּצְרַיִם בְּיָד חֲזָקָה:

21 then thou shalt say unto thy son: 'We were Pharaoh's bondmen in Egypt; and Yehovah brought us out of Egypt with a mighty hand.

כב וַיִּתֵּן יְהֹוָה אוֹתֹת וּמֹפְתִים גְּדֹלִים וְרָעִים l בְּמִצְרַיִם בְּפַרְעֹה וּבְכָל־בֵּיתוֹ לְעֵינֵינוּ:

22 And Yehovah showed signs and wonders, great and sore, upon Egypt, upon Pharaoh, and upon all his house, before our eyes.

כג וְאוֹתָנוּ הוֹצִיא מִשָּׁם לְמַעַן הָבִיא אֹתָנוּ לָתֶת לָנוּ אֶת־הָאָרֶץ אֲשֶׁר נִשְׁבַּע לַאֲבֹתֵינוּ:

23 And He brought us out from thence, that He might bring us in, to give us the land which He swore unto our fathers.

כד וַיְצַוֵּנוּ יְהֹוָה לַעֲשׂוֹת אֶת־כָּל־הַחֻקִּים הָאֵלֶּה לְיִרְאָה אֶת־יְהֹוָה אֱלֹהֵינוּ לְטוֹב לָנוּ כָּל־הַיָּמִים לְחַיֹּתֵנוּ כְּהַיּוֹם הַזֶּה:

24 And Yehovah commanded us to do all these statutes, to fear Yehovah our God, for our good always, that He might preserve us alive, as it is at this day.

כה וּצְדָקָה תִּהְיֶה־לָּנוּ כִּי־נִשְׁמֹר לַעֲשׂוֹת אֶת־כָּל־הַמִּצְוָה הַזֹּאת לִפְנֵי יְהֹוָה אֱלֹהֵינוּ כַּאֲשֶׁר צִוָּנוּ:

25 And it shall be righteousness unto us, if we observe to do all this commandment before Yehovah our God, as He hath commanded us.

[Deuteronomy 6:1-25 The Pill Tanakh]

For those who acknowledge the ancient Jewish Scriptures sourced from the Leningrad Codex as authoritative, it is clear that Deuteronomy 6, which contains the Sh'ma, associates keeping the commandments, testimonies and statues with the worship of the Almighty, יְהֹוָה Yehovah.

יז שָׁמוֹר תִּשְׁמְרוּן אֶת־מִצְוֺת יְהֹוָה אֱלֹהֵיכֶם וְעֵדֹתָיו וְחֻקָּיו אֲשֶׁר צִוָּךְ:

17 Ye shall diligently keep the commandments of Yehovah your God, and His testimonies, and His statutes, which He hath commanded thee.

[Deuteronomy 6:17 The Pill Tanakh]

The Elohim (God)
Of The Seventh–Day Sabbath

וְיוֹם֙ הַשְּׁבִיעִ֔י שַׁבָּ֖ת ׀ לַיהוָ֣ה אֱלֹהֶ֑יךָ לֹֽא־תַעֲשֶׂ֣ה
כָל־מְלָאכָ֡ה אַתָּ֣ה

but the seventh day is the sabbath unto Yehovah thy God, in it thou shalt not do any manner of work,

The foundation of worshipping יְהוָה Yehovah is observing His seventh–day Sabbath, expressed within the sixth verse of the Ten Commandments in Exodus 20 (Leningrad Codex).

זָכ֛וֹר֩ אֶת־י֥וֹם הַשַּׁבָּ֖ת לְקַדְּשֽׁ֑וֹ
שֵׁ֤שֶׁת יָמִים֙ תַּֽעֲבֹד֙ וְעָשִׂ֣יתָ
כָּל־מְלַאכְתֶּ֔ךָ וְי֨וֹם֙ הַשְּׁבִיעִ֔י
שַׁבָּ֣ת ׀ לַיהוָ֣ה אֱלֹהֶ֑יךָ לֹֽא־
תַעֲשֶׂ֣ה כָל־מְלָאכָ֡ה אַתָּ֣ה ׀
וּבִנְךָֽ־וּבִתֶּ֜ךָ עַבְדְּךָ֤ וַאֲמָֽתְךָ֙
וּבְהֶמְתֶּ֔ךָ וְגֵרְךָ֖ אֲשֶׁ֥ר בִּשְׁעָרֶֽיךָ
כִּ֣י שֵֽׁשֶׁת־יָמִים֩ עָשָׂ֨ה יְהוָ֜ה
אֶת־הַשָּׁמַ֣יִם וְאֶת־הָאָ֗רֶץ
אֶת־הַיָּם֙ וְאֶת־כָּל־אֲשֶׁר־בָּ֔ם
וַיָּ֖נַח בַּיּ֣וֹם הַשְּׁבִיעִ֑י עַל־כֵּ֗ן
בֵּרַ֧ךְ יְהוָ֛ה אֶת־י֥וֹם הַשַּׁבָּ֖ת
וַֽיְקַדְּשֵֽׁהוּ׃

20 <u>6</u> Remember the sabbath day, to keep it holy. Six days shalt thou labour, and do all thy work; but the seventh day is the sabbath unto Yehovah thy God, in it thou shalt not do any manner of work, thou, nor thy son, nor thy daughter, nor thy man-servant, nor thy maid-servant, nor thy cattle, nor thy stranger that is within thy gates; for in six days Yehovah made heaven and earth, the sea, and all that in them is, and rested on the seventh day; wherefore Yehovah blessed the sabbath day, and hallowed it.

[Exodus 20:6 The Pill Tanakh]

It is evident to me that the Christian God **"Jesus" is NOT** יְהֹוָה **[Yehovah] and neither is the Muslim God "Allah"** יְהֹוָה **[Yehovah]!** They are *different Gods!*

When יְהֹוָה *[Yehovah] said very clearly:*

כ וּ זָכוֹר אֶת־יוֹם הַשַּׁבָּת לְקַדְּשׁוֹ שֵׁשֶׁת יָמִים
תַּעֲבֹד וְעָשִׂיתָ כָּל־מְלַאכְתֶּךָ וְיוֹם הַשְּׁבִיעִי שַׁבָּת ׀
לַיהֹוָה אֱלֹהֶיךָ לֹא־תַעֲשֶׂה כָל־מְלָאכָה

"Remember the sabbath day, to keep it holy. Six days shalt thou labour, and do all thy work; but the seventh day is the sabbath unto Yehovah thy God, in it thou shalt not do any manner of work,"

He distinguished Himself from all other Gods!

יְהֹוָה **[Yehovah] did not allow the children of Israel to just interpret His words to mean something they do not mean! Theirs was to hear and obey,** not to conclude that *any day could serve as Sabbath,* including the first day of the week,

Sunday, as most Christians observe; *not to say that He does not rest because He is the creator,* so we can pray and worship on Friday, as the Islamists do.

Keeping the seventh-day Sabbath is the acknowledgement and recognition that יְהֺוָה [Yehovah] <u>is the One True God</u>, and there is no other!

Acknowledging, recognizing and observing any other day than the seventh day as the Sabbath (or day of worship) should be considered to be an expression of <u>worshipping a different God</u> other than יְהֺוָה [Yehovah]!

Epilogue

As with my previous books, I didn't start writing unless I had an overwhelming sense to do so. Please understand that doesn't mean that I consider that I am somehow a prophet. It is just that from the writing of the first book to this one, not unless I am so moved to write do I begin. Also, I pray about any effort I take on. After starting, I have been driven to bring the works to completion.

My motivation has not been monetary. From the beginning of the first book self–published in 2021 I had the sense that even if the book was meant for only one person, that may be the reason for it!

I'll admit that my second book, published in three volumes, "The PIII Tanakh — Hebrew–English Jewish Scriptures," may have been for me particularly! As I intend to read the Scriptures daily, I have a reading plan that takes me through the Jewish Scriptures in a year. **I absolutely enjoy reading from The Pill Tanakh!** Prior to its publication in 2022, I regularly read Hebrew and English from "The Stone Edition Tanach" and "The Koren Tanakh."

When I started this particular book, I was struck with thinking about the idea of the Cohen Gadol, the Jewish High Priest. That's what my intent was at the start, and "The Cohen Gadol" was the first working title. As I continued, I prayed often about not only if I should continue but also for insights into what to write.

In the process I ended up covering a variety of subjects, intending to modify ideas from previous chapters when I began a new one.

Beginning with "The Eternal Covenant" I stressed the covenant of circumcision, noting that Isaac was the first son born under that covenant. He was conceived after Abraham had been circumcised at the age of 99. The Israelite people, through succession of circumcised males, are the progenitors of the covenant of circumcision between יְהֹוָה [Yehovah] and Abraham!

In the second chapter, **"The Cohen Gadol,"** I wrote about the Jewish High Priesthood. I provided a table of all known High Priests and I also spoke about the several times that the office of the High Priest was corrupted and compromised.

I ended the chapter with a discussion about current efforts in Israel to prepare for rebuilding the Temple and also a reinstitution of the office of the Jewish High Priesthood.

In the third chapter, **"Abrahamic Religion,"** I was moved to talk about the three major Abrahamic religions, Judaism, Christianity and Islam. After providing a couple of definitions of "religion," I started a section with a quote titled **"Three Religions — One God."** I discussed all three religions.

Later, I added a heading **"Three Religions — THREE GODS!"**

Therein I claim that **Jesus in NOT יְהֹוָה [Yehovah]** and **Allah is not יְהֹוָה [Yehovah]!** I focussed on the fourth commandment, completing the discussion with the statement, **Keeping the seventh-day Sabbath is the acknowledgement and recognition that יְהֹוָה [Yehovah] is the One True God, and there is no other!**

Next, I was moved to write about prophecy, which I covered in two chapters, **"Ancient Prophecy"** and **"Head Of Gold."** In addition to giving Jewish views, I also discussed views of Christianity and Islam on some of the better known ancient prophecies.

Continuing, I wanted to add to the idea of leadership within the Israelite community, which turned into my longest chapter, **"Judges, Kings, Prophets,"** showing dates and times. I realize that may sound a bit mundane, but this chapter is a reference work which helps to understand events in ancient Israel by correlating the interrelationships and times of their occurrence.

It seemed logical to add the chapter **"Seek Yehovah,"** which, with minor changes, I borrowed from my last book, "Ad Mashiach Nagid — The Messiah In Daniel 9." As the title of the chapter expresses, worship and our daily lives should be focussed on seeking the creator of all things with all of our soul and might.

"Seek Yehovah," begins with a quote from Isaiah 55:6, *Seek ye Yehovah while He may be found.* I spoke of **repentance,**

which is founded upon having a relationship with Yehovah by turning (or returning) to Him with sincere humility.

I began the end of **"Seek Yehovah,"** with the iconic passage from Zephaniah 3:9 which speaks of turning people to a pure language – the Hebrew language being inferred: **3 9 For then will I turn to the peoples a pure language, that they may all call upon the name of Yehovah, to serve Him with one consent.**

Having knowledge of the ancient Hebrew is critical in understanding the text. I provided tables displaying Hebrew letters and vowels, ending with a brief discussion of Hebrew cantillation.

In **"The Kingdom Of Heaven"** I wanted to stress that Heaven is distinctly the realm of the Almighty. *We are earth bound!*

The ancient Jewish Scriptures often declare the greatness of Yehovah, also directing His people to worship Him by observing His statutes, ordinances and commandments, and to love Him with all our heart and all our soul.

10 12 And now, Israel, what doth Yehovah thy God require of thee, but to fear Yehovah thy God, to walk in all His ways, and to love Him, and to serve Yehovah thy God with all thy heart and with all thy soul;

13 to keep the commandments of Yehovah, and His statutes, which I command thee this day, for thy good?

14 Behold, unto Yehovah thy God belongeth the heaven, and the heaven of heavens, the earth, with all that therein is.

[Deuteronomy 10:12-14 The Pill Tanakh]

In **"The End Of The Matter"** I wanted to add to **"Seek Yehovah"** showing that our duty is to focus our lives and our worship in the service of the Creator and King of the Universe!

Early in that chapter I first quoted Deuteronomy 6:4 (**The Sh'ma**).

ד שְׁמַע יִשְׂרָאֵל יְהֹוָה אֱלֹהֵינוּ יְהֹוָה | אֶחָד:

4 Hear, O Israel: Yehovah our God, Yehovah is one.

I finished that chapter with the section called "**The Elohim (God) Of The Seventh–Day Sabbath.**"

יְהֹוָה **[Yehovah] did not allow the children of Israel to just interpret His words to mean something they do not mean! Theirs was to hear and obey,** not to conclude that *any day could serve as Sabbath,* including the first day of the week, Sunday, as most Christians observe; *not to say that He does not rest because He is the creator,* so we can pray and worship on Friday, as the Islamists do.

Keeping the seventh-day Sabbath is the acknowledgement and recognition that יְהֹוָה **[Yehovah]** is the One True God, and there is no other!

Acknowledging, recognizing and observing **any other day than the seventh day as the Sabbath (or day of worship) should be considered to be an expression of** worshipping a different God — **other than** יְהֹוָה **[Yehovah]!**

10 **12 And now, Israel, what doth Yehovah thy God require of thee, but to fear Yehovah thy God, to walk in all His ways, and to love Him, and to serve Yehovah thy God with all thy heart and with all thy soul;**

13 to keep the commandments of Yehovah, and His statutes, which I command thee this day, for thy good?

14 Behold, unto Yehovah thy God belongeth the heaven, and the heaven of heavens, the earth, with all that therein is.

[Deuteronomy 10:12-14 The Pill Tanakh]

www.ingramcontent.com/pod-product-compliance
Lightning Source LLC
Chambersburg PA
CBHW070930130626
46555CB00001B/368